THE PRIVATE PAY PRACTITIONERS WORKBOOK

Companion to The Private Pay Practitioners Playbook

Your 90-Day Implementation Guide

By D.J. Burr, LMHC, LPC

COPYRIGHT PAGE

Copyright © 2026 by D.J. Burr

All rights reserved. No part of this publication may be reproduced, distributed, or transmitted in any form or by any means without prior written permission.

For permission requests, contact: djprivatepay@gmail.com

ISBN: 979-8-9999285-3-5

Disclaimer: This workbook is for educational purposes only. It is not a substitute for professional consultation, supervision, or legal advice. Adapt all strategies to your individual circumstances and local regulations.

For more resources:
- Website: www.privatepaypractitioners.com
- Patreon: patreon.com/privatepay
- Facebook: Private Pay Practitioners & Black Private Pay Practitioners

---

HOW TO USE THIS WORKBOOK

This isn't a journal. It's a construction manual.

What's New in the Workbook

This workbook is designed to stand alone OR work alongside *The Private Pay Practitioners Playbook*. If you have the Playbook, you already have the frameworks. This workbook helps you implement them.

What's different here:

- **Two rate calculation methods** - Build up from expenses OR work down from your income goal. The Playbook introduced one approach; here you get both, plus a comparison tool.
- **Updated pricing formulas** - Based on real workshop feedback and coaching sessions, we've refined the calculations to better account for taxes and business expenses.
- **More fill-in exercises** - Less reading, more doing. Every concept has a worksheet attached.
- **90-day implementation timeline** - A structured path from "thinking about it" to "doing it."

Here's how this works:

What You'll Do:
- Work through one chapter section per week
- Complete the exercises (don't skip—each one builds on the last)
- Take action immediately on what you create
- Track your progress and adjust as needed

What You'll Create:
- Your complete private pay business plan
- All the scripts and templates you need to operate
- A 90-day implementation timeline
- Your exit strategy from insurance (if applicable)

What You'll Need:
- The Private Pay Practitioners Playbook (the book)
- 90 days of commitment
- Willingness to do the work
- A calendar and accountability system

The Timeline:
- Week 1-2: Foundation (Chapters 1-2 + Insurance Exit Roadmap)
- Week 3-4: Marketing & Client Experience (Chapters 3-4)
- Week 5-6: Growth Systems (Chapters 5-7)
- Week 7-8: Scaling & Implementation (Chapters 8-9)

You can work faster or slower—but commit to finishing.

Private pay isn't a dream. It's a decision.

This workbook helps you make it real. You don't need the Playbook to use this workbook. But if you have both, you'll move faster.

Let's build.

TABLE OF CONTENTS

Introduction	7
Chapter 1: The Private Pay Decision	11
Myth-Busting Worksheet	12
Current Reality Check: Income Calculator	14
Private Pay Projection	16
The Gross Vs. Net Reality Check	18
Experience & Market Adjustments	20
Decision Matrix	23
Fear Inventory	25
Your Decision Point	28
Your 90-Day Transition Plan	29
Chapter 2: Know Your Why & Your Who	53
Your Why Statement	54
Ideal Client Avatar	56
Niche Discovery	64
Voice & Positioning	67
Practice Values	71
Chapter 2: Action Items	75
Chapter 3: Messaging That Converts	77
Website Messaging Audit	78
Headline Formula Worksheet	80
Your Story Template	83
30-Day Social Media Content Planner	86
Boundary Language Scripts	91
Chapter 4: The Client Journey	95
Your Complete Client Journey Map	96
Chapter 4 Action Items	111
Chapter 5: Networking That Actually Works	113
The Coffee Chat Framework	114
Referral Tracking Worksheet	115
Email Templates For Networking	116
Scripts For Asking For Referrals	119
Chapter 5 Action Items	120
Chapter 6: Innovative Service Delivery	121
Service Menu Brainstorm	122

- Designing Your Service ... 124
- Pricing Your Service ... 126
- Logistics & Boundaries ... 127
- Chapter 6 Action Items ... 130

Chapter 7: CEO Mindset & Time Management ... 131
- Mindset Shift Inventory ... 132
- Systems That Save You Time ... 136
- Avoiding Burnout ... 138
- Chapter 7 Action Items ... 140

Chapter 8: Client Retention & Ethical Offboarding ... 143
- The Retention Decision Framework ... 144
- Handling Difficult Endings ... 146
- Building Your Referral Network ... 147
- Retaining The Right Clients ... 148
- Closure & Final Sessions ... 149
- Chapter 8 Action Items ... 150

Chapter 9: Scaling Your Impact ... 151
- Revenue Stream Ideas ... 152
- Seasonal Strategy ... 153
- Building A Team ... 155
- Your Legacy Practice ... 158
- Chapter 9 Action Items ... 161

Conclusion: Your 90-Day Action Plan ... 163
- Your 90-Day Action Plan ... 164
- Final Words ... 170

Appendix ... 171
- Essential Implementation Timeline ... 172
- Troubleshooting Guide ... 173
- Resource Links ... 175

INTRODUCTION

Your Private Pay Starting Line

Before we build anything, we need to know where you're starting from.

This isn't about judgment. It's about clarity.

You can't create a roadmap without knowing your current location.

The next three pages establish your baseline. Answer honestly. No one sees this but you.

Ready?

Let's go.

PRE-WORK ASSESSMENT
Where You Are Right Now

TODAY'S DATE: _____

Current Practice Status:
- Working in community mental health/agency
- In private practice accepting insurance
- In private practice, mix of insurance and private pay
- In private practice, all private pay
- Not yet in practice/just starting
- Other: _____

Current Caseload:
- Total clients: _____
- Insurance clients: _____
- Private pay clients: _____
- Hours per week seeing clients: _____

Current Income Reality:
- Average monthly income (before taxes): $_____
- Average hourly rate (what you actually take home): $_____
- Percentage of income from insurance: _____%
- Percentage of income from private pay: _____%

Current Satisfaction (Rate 1-10):
- Clinical work satisfaction: _____
- Income satisfaction: _____
- Schedule flexibility: _____
- Professional autonomy: _____
- Overall practice satisfaction: _____

What Brought You Here?
In one sentence, why did you buy this workbook?

_____
_____
_____
_____

YOUR WHY + COMMITMENT
Your Private Pay Why

Why NOW? What needs to change?
_____
_____
_____
_____

What will private pay give you that you don't have now?
_____
_____
_____
_____

YOUR 90-DAY COMMITMENT CONTRACT

I, _____, commit to completing this workbook and taking action on my private pay practice over the next 90 days.

I understand that:
- This requires actual work, not just reading
- I'll need to implement what I create, not just fill out worksheets
- Some exercises will feel uncomfortable—I'll do them anyway
- I'm building a business, not just wishing for one

My target completion date: _____
My accountability partner (if applicable): _____
Signature: _____ Date: _____

START DATE: _____
TARGET COMPLETION: _____ (90 days from start)

Chapter 1

The Private Pay Decision

Before you can build a private pay practice, you need to decide if it's actually right for you.

Not "someday maybe." Not "I'll think about it."

A real decision.

This chapter helps you:
- Identify which myths are keeping you stuck
- Calculate what you're ACTUALLY making now vs. what you could make
- Assess your fears honestly (and realistically)
- Make the decision with clarity, not panic

Reference: Chapter 1 in the Private Pay Practitioners Playbook
TIME TO COMPLETE: 1-2 hours

Let's start by busting some myths.

MYTH-BUSTING WORKSHEET

Which Myths Are Keeping YOU Stuck?

Check any myths you've believed (be honest):
- "Private pay is elitist—therapy should be accessible to everyone"
- "No one will pay out of pocket for therapy"
- "I need to accept insurance to have enough clients"
- "Only established therapists can go private pay"
- "I'll lose all my clients if I stop taking insurance"
- "Private pay means I don't care about people who can't afford it"
- "I'm not good enough/experienced enough to charge rates that meet my needs"
- "My area is too poor for private pay"
- "I need a full caseload before I can transition"

Now pick your TOP 3 myths that feel most true to you:
1. _____
2. _____
3. _____

For each myth, answer:

MYTH #1: _____
Why do I believe this?
_____
_____
_____
_____

What evidence do I actually have that this is true?
_____
_____
_____
_____

What would be possible if this myth WASN'T true?
_____
_____
_____

MYTH #2: _____

Why do I believe this?
_____
_____
_____
_____

What evidence do I actually have that this is true?
_____
_____
_____
_____

What would be possible if this myth WASN'T true?
_____
_____
_____
_____

MYTH #3: _____

Why do I believe this?
_____
_____
_____
_____

What evidence do I actually have that this is true?
_____
_____
_____
_____

What would be possible if this myth WASN'T true?
_____
_____
_____
_____

CURRENT REALITY CHECK: INCOME CALCULATOR
What You're ACTUALLY Making Per Hour

Let's get brutally honest about your current income.

STEP 1: YOUR GROSS INCOME

Average monthly income (before taxes): $_____
Multiply by 12: $_____ (annual gross income)

STEP 2: YOUR ACTUAL EXPENSES

- Insurance panel credentialing fees (annual): $_____
- Insurance billing service/software: $_____
- EHR/EHR system: $_____
- Malpractice insurance: $_____
- Office rent (if applicable): $_____
- Continuing education: $_____
- Professional memberships: $_____
- Marketing/website: $_____
- Other business expenses: $_____

TOTAL ANNUAL EXPENSES: $_____

STEP 3: YOUR NET INCOME

- Gross annual income: $_____
- Minus total expenses: - $_____
- **= NET ANNUAL INCOME**: $_____

Divide by 12 months: $_____ per month (net)

Private Pay Practitioners Workbook

STEP 4: YOUR ACTUAL HOURLY RATE

Hours per week seeing clients: _____ Multiply by 4.3 weeks per month: _____ (monthly client hours)

BUT WAIT—let's add the HIDDEN hours:

- Hours per week on documentation: _____
- Hours per week on insurance claims/appeals: _____
- Hours per week on scheduling/admin: _____
- Hours per week on no-shows/cancellations: _____

TOTAL HOURS PER WEEK: _____ Multiply by 4.3 weeks: _____ (total monthly hours worked)

YOUR ACTUAL HOURLY RATE:
Net monthly income ÷ Total monthly hours worked = $_____/hour

How does that feel?
_____
_____
_____

Is this sustainable?
_____
_____
_____
_____
_____

PRIVATE PAY PROJECTION
What You COULD Be Making

Now let's run the numbers for private pay.

There are two ways to calculate your minimum rate. Some people think better building UP from expenses. Others think better working DOWN from an income goal.

Do both. Then compare.

METHOD 1: BUILD UP FROM EXPENSES
This method asks: "What do I need to cover my bills and run my business?"

STEP 1: CALCULATE YOUR PERSONAL NEEDS

What do you need to EARN (after expenses) to sustain your life?

Monthly expenses (personal):
- Rent/mortgage: $_____
- Utilities: $_____
- Food: $_____
- Transportation: $_____
- Insurance (health, car, etc.): $_____
- Debt payments: $_____
- Savings goals: $_____
- Other living expenses: $_____

TOTAL MONTHLY PERSONAL EXPENSES: $_____

STEP 2: ADD YOUR BUFFER

Add 20% for taxes and unexpected expenses:
$_____ x 0.20 = $_____

Total personal expenses: $_____
Plus 20% buffer: + $_____

YOUR MONTHLY PERSONAL NEED: $_____

STEP 3: ADD YOUR BUSINESS EXPENSES

Monthly business expenses:
- Office rent (if applicable): $_____
- EMR system: $_____
- Malpractice insurance: $_____
- Website/marketing: $_____
- Continuing education (monthly avg): $_____
- Professional memberships (monthly avg): $_____
- Other expenses: $_____

TOTAL MONTHLY BUSINESS EXPENSES: $_____

STEP 4: YOUR TOTAL MONTHLY NEED

- Monthly personal need (from Step 2): $_____
- Monthly business expenses (from Step 3): + $_____

TOTAL MONTHLY NEED: $_____

STEP 5: YOUR TARGET CASELOAD

How many client sessions per week do you WANT to see? _____
(Remember: No insurance = less admin time = you can see fewer clients)
Sessions per week: _____ x 4.3 weeks = _____ sessions per month

Private Pay Practitioners Workbook

STEP 6: YOUR METHOD 1 MINIMUM RATE

Total monthly need: $_____
Divided by sessions per month: _____

METHOD 1 MINIMUM RATE: $_____
This is what you NEED to charge just to cover your bills and run your business.
METHOD 2: WORK DOWN FROM INCOME GOAL
This method asks: "What do I want to make?"

THE GROSS VS. NET REALITY CHECK

Before we calculate, understand this:

If you want to NET $100K (actual money you can spend), you need to GROSS about $130-140K.

Why? Self-employment taxes and business expenses eat 25-35% of your gross income.

This is why therapists who say "I'm making six figures!" are sometimes still struggling. They're confusing gross with net.

Let's calculate correctly.

STEP 1: YOUR INCOME GOAL

What do you want to take HOME annually?
Not gross. Not revenue. What do you want in your actual bank account to spend on your life?

My annual NET income goal: $_____

STEP 2: CONVERT TO GROSS

Multiply your NET goal by 1.35
(This accounts for approximately 25% taxes + 10% business overhead)

$_____ x 1.35 = $_____

My needed GROSS income: $_____

STEP 3: BREAK IT DOWN MONTHLY

Divide your gross income by 12 months:
$_____ ÷ 12 = $_____

My needed MONTHLY gross: $_____

STEP 4: YOUR TARGET CASELOAD

How many client sessions per week do you WANT to see? _____
Sessions per week: _____ x 4.3 weeks = _____ sessions per month

My ideal monthly sessions: _____

STEP 5: YOUR METHOD 2 MINIMUM RATE

Monthly gross need: $_____
Divided by sessions per month: _____

METHOD 2 MINIMUM RATE: $_____

COMPARE BOTH METHODS

Method 1 (expenses up): $_____
Method 2 (income goal down): $_____

WHAT THE COMPARISON TELLS YOU
- **They match or they're close** Great. Your lifestyle expenses and income goals are aligned. Your minimum rate is clear. Use either number as your baseline.
- **Method 2 is significantly higher** Your income goals are bigger than your current expenses.

Maybe you're planning for future expenses, aggressive saving, building wealth, or paying off debt faster. That's fine - just know you're aiming higher than survival.
- **Method 1 is significantly higher** Your current lifestyle costs more than your stated income goal. Something has to give:

    - Cut expenses
    - Raise your income goal
    - See more clients
    - Or accept that your "goal" was actually lower than what you need

YOUR WORKING BASELINE RATE
Based on BOTH methods, my baseline minimum rate is: $_____

Note: This calculation includes a buffer for irregular months but does not include your estimated tax burden. For a more detailed calculation that accounts for taxes, visit privatepaypractitioners.com/rate-calc

I'm using this number because:
_____
_____
_____

This is the MINIMUM you need to charge to survive and run your business.

Now let's see what you SHOULD charge based on your experience and the market.

EXPERIENCE & MARKET ADJUSTMENTS

STEP 7: ADD YOUR PROFESSIONAL EXPERIENCE

Your baseline rate only covers survival. Your experience and expertise add value.

Your experience level:
- 0-2 years: Add $20-40
- 3-5 years: Add $40-60
- 6-10 years: Add $60-80

- 10+ years: Add $80-100+

Experience adjustment: + $_____
Specialized training/certifications: (EMDR, IFS, sex therapy certification, Gottman, etc.)
Add: + $_____
Niche expertise that's in demand:
Add: + $_____

Your baseline rate: $_____
Plus experience adjustment: + $_____
Plus certifications: + $_____
Plus niche expertise: + $_____

= YOUR CALCULATED RATE: $_____

STEP 8: MARKET REALITY CHECK (NOT MARKET MATCHING)

NOW look at what others charge in your area:
- Low end in my area: $_____
- High end in my area: $_____
- Average: $_____

Your calculated rate: $_____

Compare:
- My rate is BELOW the low end (You're undercharging based on your needs - consider raising)
- My rate is in the MIDDLE range (You're positioned well)
- My rate is ABOVE the high end (Are you offering premium services that justify this?)

If your calculated rate is BELOW market average, you have room to grow.
If your calculated rate is ABOVE market high end, ask yourself:
- Do I have specialized expertise that justifies premium pricing?
- Am I targeting a specific clientele willing to pay more?
- Or do I need to adjust my lifestyle expenses or caseload?

STEP 9: YOUR FINAL PRIVATE PAY RATE

Based on YOUR needs + YOUR experience + market reality:
MY PRIVATE PAY RATE: $_____/session

Why this rate?
_____
_____
_____
_____

How does this rate feel?
- Comfortable and sustainable
- Scary but necessary
- Too low (I could charge more based on my needs)
- Too high (I need to adjust something)

YOUR PROJECTED INCOME

STEP 10: PROJECTED ANNUAL INCOME
- Sessions per week: _____
- Multiply by 4.3 weeks per month: _____ sessions per month
- Multiply by your rate: $_____ x _____ = $_____ per month (gross)
- Multiply by 12 months: $_____ x 12 = $_____/year (projected gross)
- Minus annual business expenses: - $_____

= PROJECTED NET ANNUAL INCOME: $_____
Divide by 12 months: $_____/month (net)

Does this meet your needs?
- Yes, this works
- No, I need to adjust: _____

STEP 11: YOUR PROJECTED HOURLY RATE

- Client hours per week: _____
- Admin hours per week (estimate 3-5 hours): _____
- **TOTAL HOURS PER WEEK**: _____

Multiply by 4.3 weeks: _____ hours per month
Projected net monthly income ÷ Total monthly hours = $_____ **/hour**

THE COMPARISON

- Current actual hourly rate: $_____
- Projected private pay hourly rate: $_____
- **Difference**: $_____

What does this tell you?
_____
_____
_____
_____

DECISION MATRIX
Stay With Insurance vs. Go Private Pay

Rate each factor 1-10 (1 = terrible, 10 = excellent)

	INSURANCE (current)	PRIVATE PAY (projected)
Income potential		
Schedule flexibility		
Administrative burden		
Clinical autonomy		
Client selection		
Job satisfaction		

Professional growth		
Work/life balance		
Financial stability		
Alignment with values		
TOTAL SCORE:		

DEAL-BREAKERS:

What would make staying with insurance impossible?
_____
_____
_____
_____

What would make private pay impossible?
_____
_____
_____
_____

REALISTIC CONCERNS:
What are your THREE biggest concerns about going private pay?
1. _____
2. _____
3. _____

For each concern, ask: Is this a REAL obstacle or a FEAR?
1. Real obstacle / Fear (circle one) If real, what would need to happen to overcome it?
   _____
   _____
   _____

2. Real obstacle / Fear (circle one) If real, what would need to happen to overcome it?

_____
_____
_____
_____

3. Real obstacle / Fear (circle one) If real, what would need to happen to overcome it?
_____
_____
_____
_____
_____

FEAR INVENTORY

What Are You Actually Afraid Of?

Rate each fear 1-10 (1 = not afraid at all, 10 = terrified)
- I won't have enough clients _____
- People won't pay my rates _____
- I'll lose all my current clients _____
- I'll run out of money _____
- I'm not experienced enough _____
- I'm not good enough _____
- People will think I'm greedy _____
- I'll be judged by other therapists _____
- My practice will fail _____
- I'll have to go back to agency work _____
- I won't be able to help people who can't afford therapy _____
- 'll be lonely without colleagues _____
- Other: _____

Pick your TOP 3 fears (highest rated):
1. _____
2. _____
3. _____

REALITY-TESTING YOUR FEARS:

FEAR #1:
___

What's the WORST that could actually happen?
___
___
___
___

How likely is that? (be honest) ____%
If it happened, what would you do?
___
___
___
___

What's the BEST that could happen?
___
___
___
___

How likely is that? ____%
What's the MOST LIKELY outcome?
___
___
___
___

FEAR #2:
___

What's the WORST that could actually happen?
___
___
___
___

How likely is that? _____%
If it happened, what would you do?
_____
_____
_____
_____

What's the BEST that could happen?
_____
_____
_____
_____

How likely is that? _____%
What's the MOST LIKELY outcome?
_____
_____
_____
_____

FEAR #3:
_____

What's the WORST that could actually happen?
_____
_____
_____
_____

How likely is that? _____%
If it happened, what would you do?
_____
_____
_____
_____

What's the BEST that could happen?
_____
_____
_____

How likely is that? ____%
What's the MOST LIKELY outcome?
_____
_____
_____
_____

YOUR DECISION POINT

Based on everything you just worked through:

Circle one:
I'M READY TO GO PRIVATE PAY → Move to the Insurance Exit Roadmap
I NEED MORE INFORMATION → What specific questions do you still have?
_____
_____

I'M NOT READY YET → What needs to happen first?
_____
_____

IF YOU'RE READY:
Your commitment: I will transition to private pay by _____
Your first step: _____
Who will hold you accountable? _____

IF YOU'RE NOT READY:
That's okay. But answer this:
What would need to change for you to be ready?

When will you revisit this decision? _____

NEXT STEPS:
- If transitioning from insurance → Go to Insurance Exit Roadmap
- If already private pay or starting fresh → Skip to Chapter 2
- If still deciding → Set a date to complete this chapter again
-

YOUR 90-DAY TRANSITION PLAN

If you're reading this section, you've made the decision.

Now comes the execution.

Leaving insurance panels isn't something you do on a whim. It requires planning, preparation, and a clear timeline.

This roadmap gives you the step-by-step process for exiting insurance panels while maintaining your income and protecting your clients.

You'll learn:
- How to prepare financially before giving notice
- What to communicate to clients (and when)
- How to handle existing authorizations
- Scripts for difficult conversations
- What to do in your first 90 days post-insurance
- How to troubleshoot common problems

THREE EXIT PATHS:

- **FULL EXIT**: Leave all insurance panels, go 100% private pay
- **PARTIAL EXIT**: Keep 1-2 preferred panels, go private pay for the rest
- **GRADUAL TRANSITION**: Phase out insurance over 6-12 months

Choose your path, then follow the timeline that works for you.
Let's start with preparation.

Private Pay Practitioners Workbook

PRE-EXIT PREPARATION (30-60 DAYS BEFORE)
What to Do BEFORE You Give Notice

This is the foundation. Don't skip this phase.

FINANCIAL PREPARATION

Calculate your financial buffer
How much money do you need saved to feel secure during transition?
- 3 months of expenses: $_____
- 6 months of expenses: $_____
- Current savings: $_____
- Amount needed: $_____

Can you start transition now?
- Yes
- No, need to save first

Review your current insurance contracts
Do any require specific notice periods? (Check each panel)
- Panel name: _____ Notice required: ____ days
- Panel name: _____ Notice required: ____ days
- Panel name: _____ Notice required: ____ days
- Panel name: _____ Notice required: ____ days

Identify current authorizations and end dates
How many clients have active authorizations? _____
What are the end dates? (List any ending in next 90 days)
_____
_____
_____

Decide your private pay rate (you did this in Chapter 1)

My private pay rate: $_____

Set your transition date
Target date to stop accepting insurance: _____

CLIENT INVENTORY

Current insurance clients: _____

For each insurance client, ask yourself:

LIKELY TO TRANSITION TO PRIVATE PAY:
- Has expressed dissatisfaction with insurance limitations
- Has financial means (you think)
- Values the work and is committed to therapy
- Would benefit from continued treatment

Number who might transition: _____

LIKELY TO NEED REFERRALS:
- Truly cannot afford private pay
- Would do fine with another insurance-accepting provider
- Is near end of treatment anyway
- Expressed concerns about cost in the past

Number who'll need referrals: _____

UNCLEAR:
- Haven't discussed finances
- Might be able to afford it but unsure
- Need to have the conversation

Number unclear: _____

SYSTEMS PREPARATION

- Research superbill templates (You'll provide these to clients who want to submit to insurance)
- Set up Square, Stripe, or other payment processing Platform you'll use: _____
- Update your EHR/practice management system Does it support private pay?

- Yes
- No, need new system
- Update your website (if applicable) Does it mention insurance?
  - Yes, needs updating
  - No
- Prepare your new client paperwork Does it reference insurance panels?
  - Yes, needs updating
  - No
- Create your referral list for clients you'll transition 3-5 therapists who accept insurance in your area:

1. _____ Specialties: _____
2. _____ Specialties: _____
3. _____ Specialties: _____
4. _____ Specialties: _____
5. _____ Specialties: _____

LEGAL/COMPLIANCE PREPARATION

- Review termination clauses in insurance contracts. Any penalties for leaving?
  - Yes
  - No
- Consult with a healthcare attorney (if concerned). Scheduled consultation?
  - Yes
  - No
  - Not needed
- Understand your state's regulations about superbills
- Prepare for CAQH profile updates (deactivation)

MINDSET PREPARATION

What are you most worried about with this transition?

_____
_____
_____
_____

Who can support you during this process?
_____
_____
_____

What's your backup plan if it doesn't go as expected?
_____
_____
_____
_____

ONCE ALL BOXES ARE CHECKED, YOU'RE READY TO GIVE NOTICE.

THE NOTICE PERIOD (30-90 DAYS)
Communicating Your Decision

You've done the prep work. Now it's time to tell people.

STEP 1: SUBMIT FORMAL NOTICE TO INSURANCE PANELS

When to submit: _____ (based on required notice periods)

What to include in your notice:
- Effective termination date
- Your NPI number
- Request for confirmation of termination
- Request for final claims payment timeline

Use this template (customize as needed):

INSURANCE TERMINATION LETTER TEMPLATE

[Date]

[Insurance Company Name] Provider Relations Department [Address]

RE: Notice of Termination from Provider Panel NPI: [Your NPI Number] Provider Name: [Your Name] Tax ID: [Your Tax ID]

Dear Provider Relations,

I am writing to provide formal notice of my termination from [Insurance Company Name]'s provider panel, effective [Date - typically 30-90 days from notice date, per contract requirements].

Please confirm receipt of this notice and provide information regarding:
- Final date I may see patients under this contract
- Timeline for final claims submission
- Expected payment schedule for outstanding claims
- Process for panel deactivation

Please send confirmation to: [Your Email] [Your Phone Number]

Thank you for your assistance with this transition.

Sincerely, [Your Signature] [Your Printed Name] [License Number]

- Panel 1 notice submitted: _____ Confirmation received: _____
- Panel 2 notice submitted: _____ Confirmation received: _____
- Panel 3 notice submitted: _____ Confirmation received: _____
- Panel 4 notice submitted: _____ Confirmation received: _____

STEP 2: COMMUNICATE WITH CURRENT CLIENTS

Timeline for client communication:
- 60 days before transition: Inform clients in session (individually)
- 45 days before: Send written notice/email (if appropriate)
- 30 days before: Follow-up conversations about their options
- 2 weeks before: Final confirmation of their decision

IN-SESSION SCRIPT: INFORMING CLIENTS

"I want to let you know about a change in my practice. Starting [date], I'll no longer be accepting [insurance name]. This means if you'd like to continue working together, sessions would be private pay at $[rate] per session.

I can provide you with a superbill that you can submit to your insurance for potential out-of-network reimbursement. I can't predict what your specific plan will cover, so I recommend calling them to ask about your out-of-network benefits.

I know this is a big change. I want to make sure you have time to think about what works best for you. We have [X weeks] to figure out the right plan.

Your options are:
- Continue with me at the private pay rate
- I can refer you to another therapist who accepts your insurance
- We can work together to create a transition plan that makes sense

What questions do you have?"

COMMON CLIENT RESPONSES & HOW TO HANDLE THEM:

"I can't afford that."
Your response: "I completely understand. Let me give you some referrals to excellent therapists who accept your insurance. I want to make sure you continue getting support."

"Can you make an exception for me?"
Your response: "I appreciate our work together. Unfortunately, I'm making this change across my entire practice for sustainability reasons. I can't make exceptions. Let's explore what would work best for you."

"Will insurance reimburse me if I submit a superbill?"
Your response: "That depends on your specific plan. I'd recommend calling the number on the back of your insurance card and asking about out-of-network benefits. I can provide the superbill,

but I can't guarantee or predict what your plan will cover."

"How long do I have to decide?"
Your response: "We have [X weeks] until the change takes effect. Let's plan to make a decision by [date] so we have time to create a good transition if needed."

"This feels sudden."
Your response: "I know changes can feel unsettling. I'm giving you [X weeks] notice so you have time to make the best decision for yourself. I'm here to support whatever you choose."

WRITTEN NOTICE TEMPLATE (EMAIL/LETTER)

Subject: Important Update About My Practice

Dear [Client Name],

I wanted to follow up on our recent conversation about changes to my practice.
Starting [Date], I will no longer be accepting [Insurance Name]. If you would like to continue our work together, sessions will be $[Rate] per session, and I can provide superbills for potential insurance reimbursement.

Your options:
- Continue therapy with me at the private pay rate of $[Rate]
- Transition to another therapist who accepts your insurance (I'm happy to provide referrals)
- Take a break from therapy at this time

I value our work together and want to support you in whatever decision makes the most sense for you. Please let me know your preference by [Date] so we can plan accordingly.

If you have questions, we can discuss them in our next session or you can email me.

Best, [Your Name]

TRACKING CLIENT DECISIONS

Create a simple spreadsheet to track:

Client Name	Insurance	Decision	Follow-up Needed	Notes

Decisions:
- Transitioning to private pay
- Needs referral
- Still deciding
- Ending therapy

FIRST 90 DAYS POST-INSURANCE

What to Expect & What to Do

You've given notice. Clients have made decisions. Now what?

MONTH 1: TRANSITION & ADJUSTMENT

WEEK 1-2: THE IMMEDIATE AFTERMATH
What will happen:
- Some clients will transition smoothly to private pay
- Some clients will terminate (and that's okay)
- Your caseload will likely drop initially
- You'll feel panic (this is normal)
- You'll question your decision (also normal)

What to do:
- Process final insurance claims immediately. Track submission dates and expected payments
- Follow up on outstanding payments
- Activate your marketing (NOW is the time)
- Update website to remove insurance references
- Post on social media about accepting new clients
- Email your professional network
- Reach out to referral sources
- Fill your schedule strategically. Don't panic-fill with clients who aren't your ideal fit
- Track your numbers weekly
    - New inquiries: _____
    - Consultations scheduled: _____
    - New clients started: _____
    - Current caseload: _____
    - Monthly income: $_____

WEEK 3-4: BUILDING MOMENTUM

What to do:
- Offer consultation calls to all inquiries
- Perfect your consultation script (see Chapter 4)
- Network actively: Coffee meetings, professional events, online connections
- Create content that attracts your ideal clients: Blog posts, social media, newsletter
- Monitor your emotional state: Loneliness? Find a consultation group. Anxiety about money? Review your numbers objectively. Regret? Remember why you made this decision.

MONTH 2: STABILIZATION

What to expect:
- New client flow should be increasing
- You're getting better at consultations
- Private pay starts feeling more normal
- Financial anxiety may still be present (normal)

What to do:
- Evaluate what marketing is working. Where are your new clients coming from?
- Double down on what's working
- Adjust rates if needed (but don't drop them in panic)
- Refine your ideal client description: Who's thriving in your practice? Get more of them.
- Build systems to reduce admin time: Templates, automated scheduling, streamlined

processes
- Continue networking consistently: At least 2-3 professional connections per week

MONTH 3: GROWTH MODE

What to expect:
- Caseload is rebuilding
- Income is stabilizing
- You're more confident in consultations
- Private pay feels more sustainable

What to do:
- Assess your 90-day results
    - Starting caseload: _____
    - Current caseload: _____
    - Starting monthly income: $_____
    - Current monthly income: $_____
    - New clients added: _____
    - Conversion rate: _____%
- Identify what's working and what needs adjustment

Working well:
_____
_____
_____

Needs improvement:
_____
_____
_____
_____

- Plan for next quarter
    - Income goal: $_____
    - Caseload goal: _____
    - Marketing priorities: _____

- Consider adding innovative services Groups, intensives, workshops (see Chapter 6)

90-DAY FINANCIAL TRACKER

Track these numbers WEEKLY:

	Week 1	Week 2	Week 3	Week 4	Monthly Total
New inquiries					
Consultations					
New clients					
Sessions held					
Gross income					
Expenses					
Net income					

Repeat for Months 2 and 3.

This gives you REAL DATA instead of anxiety-driven assumptions.

COMMON EXIT SCENARIOS

Choose Your Path

Not everyone exits insurance the same way. Here are the three most common approaches:

SCENARIO 1: FULL EXIT (All Insurance → All Private Pay)

Best for:
- Therapists burned out on insurance hassles
- Those with strong referral networks
- Practitioners with specialized niches
- Therapists with a financial buffer

Timeline: 30-90 days

Process:
1. Give notice to ALL panels simultaneously
2. Inform all clients at once
3. Complete transition by target date
4. Focus 100% on private pay marketing

Pros:
- Clean break, clear messaging
- No confusion about who you accept
- Full autonomy immediately

Cons:
- Biggest initial income drop
- Highest risk if marketing doesn't work
- Can't go back easily

SCENARIO 2: PARTIAL EXIT (Keep 1-2 Preferred Panels)

Best for:
- Therapists wanting to maintain some insurance access
- Those concerned about serving specific populations
- Practitioners testing private pay waters
- Therapists in areas where insurance is necessary for accessibility

Timeline: 30-90 days for initial exit, ongoing hybrid model

Process:
1. Identify 1-2 panels with best reimbursement rates/least hassle
2. Exit all other panels
3. Accept new insurance clients selectively
4. Market private pay as primary option

Pros:
- Income safety net
- Serve clients who truly need insurance
- Test private pay without full commitment

Cons:
- Still dealing with some insurance admin
- Mixed messaging to potential clients
- Can't fully escape insurance limitations

Which 1-2 panels will you keep?
Panel 1: _____ Why this one? _____
Panel 2: _____ Why this one? _____

SCENARIO 3: GRADUAL TRANSITION (Phase Out Over 6-12 Months)

Best for:
- Therapists with full insurance caseloads
- Those needing to build private pay slowly
- Practitioners with financial constraints
- Therapists wanting to minimize client disruption

Timeline: 6-12 months

Process:
1. Stop accepting NEW insurance clients (keep existing)
2. Fill new openings with private pay only
3. As insurance clients naturally terminate, replace with private pay
4. Give formal exit notice once caseload is mostly private pay

Month-by-month example:

Month 1: 20 insurance clients, 0 private pay
- Stop taking insurance referrals, start marketing private pay
- Month 3: 18 insurance clients, 3 private pay
- Continue marketing, 2 insurance clients terminated

Month 6: 12 insurance clients, 8 private pay
- Halfway there, momentum building

Month 9: 6 insurance clients, 12 private pay
- Give notice to insurance panels

Month 12: 0 insurance clients, 15-20 private pay
- Fully transitioned

Pros:
- Lowest financial risk

- Maintains relationships with current clients
- Time to build private pay skills
- Can adjust strategy as you go

Cons:
- Takes longer to achieve full autonomy
- Still dealing with insurance for months
- Requires patience and discipline
- Can lose motivation over long timeline

YOUR CHOSEN PATH:
- Full Exit - Target date: _____
- Partial Exit - Keeping panels: _____
- Gradual Transition - Target completion: _____

Why this path makes sense for you:

_____
_____
_____
_____
_____
_____
_____
_____

ESSENTIAL SCRIPTS
Word-For-Word Language for Difficult Conversations
Copy these. Customize them. Use them.

SCRIPT 1: CLIENT NOTIFICATION (IN-SESSION)

For clients who can likely afford private pay:
"I want to share an update about my practice. Starting [date], I'm transitioning away from accepting [insurance name]. This change allows me to focus on providing the best possible care without insurance limitations.

For you, this means if you'd like to continue working together, sessions would be $[rate] per session. I can provide a superbill that you can submit to your insurance for potential reimbursement as an out-of-network provider. I can't predict what your specific plan will cover, so I recommend calling them to ask about your out-of-network benefits.

I know this is a change. I want you to have time to think about what makes sense for you. We have [X weeks] to figure this out together.
What questions do you have?"

For clients who likely cannot afford private pay:
"I want to let you know about a change in my practice. Starting [date], I'm no longer going to be accepting [insurance name].

I know private pay isn't feasible for everyone. I want to make sure you continue getting good care. I have referrals for excellent therapists who accept your insurance and who I think would be a good fit for you.

We have [X weeks] to create a good transition plan. How does that sound?"

SCRIPT 2: RESPONDING TO "I CAN'T AFFORD THAT"

"I completely understand. Therapy is an investment, and I want you to be able to continue getting support. Let me give you a few names of therapists I respect who accept your insurance. I'll also write you a brief transition summary so they have context about our work together.

Would you like me to help you get connected with someone?"

SCRIPT 3: RESPONDING TO "CAN YOU MAKE AN EXCEPTION?"

"I really value the work we've done together. I'm making this change across my entire practice because it's what I need for sustainability. I wish I could make exceptions, but I can't maintain a practice where I'm charging different rates for different clients.

I want to support you in making the decision that's right for you. Would continuing at the private pay rate work for you, or would a referral to another therapist be better?"

SCRIPT 4: RESPONDING TO "THIS FEELS SUDDEN"

"I hear that changes can feel unsettling, especially when you're already dealing with [their therapeutic issues]. I'm giving you [X weeks] notice specifically so this doesn't have to be rushed. We have time to talk through your options and make a plan that feels right. Our work together doesn't have to end if you don't want it to, but I also want to make sure whatever you decide feels sustainable for you.
What would feel most supportive right now?"

SCRIPT 5: INSURANCE COMPANY TERMINATION CALL FOLLOW-UP

When they ask why you're leaving:

"I'm restructuring my practice to focus on private pay services. I'd like to confirm my termination date and understand the process for final claims submission."

(Keep it brief. Don't over-explain. They don't need your life story.)

SCRIPT 6: CONSULTATION CALL (FOR NEW PRIVATE PAY INQUIRIES)

"Thanks for reaching out. I'd love to learn more about what brings you to therapy and see if we might be a good fit.

Just so you know upfront, I'm a private pay practice, which means I don't accept insurance directly. My rate is $[rate] per session. I can provide superbills if you have out-of-network benefits, but I can't guarantee what your insurance will cover.

Does that work for you, or are you specifically looking for someone who accepts insurance in-network?"

(Qualify them early. Don't waste time on consultations with people who need insurance.)

SCRIPT 7: REFERRAL TRANSITION CONVERSATION

"We've been working together for [timeframe], and I think you've made great progress. Given the insurance change and what makes sense financially for you, I think it's a good time to transition your care.

I'd like to refer you to [name], who specializes in [relevant area] and accepts your insurance. I'll provide them with a summary of our work so you don't have to start from scratch.
Before we end, I want to make sure we have closure on the work we've done together. What's been most helpful for you in our sessions?"

(Create a clean ending. Don't just hand them a name and disappear.)

SCRIPT 8: NETWORKING ANNOUNCEMENT (TO REFERRAL SOURCES)

Email template:

Subject: Practice Update - Now Accepting New Private Pay Clients

Hi [Name],

I wanted to let you know about a change in my practice. As of [date], I'm transitioning to private pay and have a few openings for new clients.

I'm continuing to specialize in [your niche], and I'm looking for clients who are [ideal client description].

My rate is $[rate] per session, and I provide superbills for clients who want to submit for out-of-network reimbursement.

If you come across anyone who might be a good fit, I'd appreciate the referral. Happy to chat more about the types of clients I work best with.

Thanks for your continued support, [Your Name]

Use these scripts as starting points. Make them sound like YOU.

SUPERBILL SETUP

Helping Clients Get Reimbursed

A superbill is a detailed receipt that clients can submit to their insurance for out-of-network reimbursement.

You're not billing insurance. You're giving clients a form THEY can use.

WHAT A SUPERBILL MUST INCLUDE:

Your information:
- Full name and credentials
- NPI number
- Tax ID (EIN) or SSN
- License number and state
- Practice address
- Phone number

Client information:
- Full name
- Date of birth
- Address

Service information:
- Date of service
- CPT code (90791 for intake, 90834/90837/90853 for sessions)
- Diagnosis code (ICD-10)
- Amount charged
- Amount paid

Your signature

Private Pay Practitioners Workbook

SAMPLE SUPERBILL TEMPLATE:

[Your Practice Name] [Your Name, Credentials] [Address] [Phone] | [Email] NPI: [Number] | Tax ID: [Number] | License: [Number]

CLIENT INFORMATION:

Name: _____ Date of Birth: _____ Address: _____ Insurance ID: _____

SERVICE DETAILS:

Date of Service	CPT Code	Diagnosis (ICD-10)	Fee	Paid

Total Charges: $_____ Total Paid: $_____

Provider Signature: _____ Date: _____

COMMON CPT CODES FOR THERAPISTS:

- 90791 - Psychiatric diagnostic evaluation (intake session)
- 90832 - Psychotherapy, 30 minutes
- 90834 - Psychotherapy, 45 minutes (most common for weekly therapy)
- 90837 - Psychotherapy, 60 minutes
- 90846 - Family therapy without patient present
- 90847 - Family therapy with patient present

- 90853 - Group therapy

HOW TO PROVIDE SUPERBILLS TO CLIENTS:

Option 1: Monthly batch. Generate superbills once per month for each client, email or hand to them
Option 2: Per session, provide a superbill after each session (more admin work)
Option 3: Client portal. Use your EHR to make superbills available for download

Recommended: Option 1 or 3 (less admin burden on you)

IMPORTANT DISCLAIMERS:

- Never guarantee reimbursement amounts
- Make it clear you're not responsible for claim denials
- Tell clients to verify their out-of-network benefits BEFORE starting
- You are not submitting claims - they are

LANGUAGE TO USE WITH CLIENTS:

"I provide superbills that you can submit to your insurance for potential out-of-network reimbursement. I recommend calling your insurance company first to ask about your out-of-network mental health benefits. Ask them specifically:

- Do I have out-of-network benefits for mental health?
- What percentage is covered?
- Do I need to meet a deductible first?
- How do I submit a claim?

I can't guarantee what they'll reimburse or predict what your plan will cover. Your insurance company can give you that information directly."

WHERE TO CREATE SUPERBILLS:

- SimplePractice (built-in superbill feature)
- TherapyNotes (built-in superbill feature)
- Healthie (built-in superbill feature)
- Google Docs/Microsoft Word template (manual)
- Superbill apps like Mentaya or Reimbursify (they help clients submit)

My superbill system: _____

TROUBLESHOOTING GUIDE
When Things Don't Go As Planned

Problem: My caseload dropped significantly and I'm panicking.
Solution:
- First, check the timeline. If it's been less than 60 days, this is normal. It takes time to rebuild.
- Review your marketing. Are you actually doing it consistently?
- Assess your consultation skills. Are you converting inquiries to clients?
- Check your messaging. Does your website clearly communicate who you help and how?
- Don't drop your rates in panic. Hold steady for at least 90 days.

Problem: Clients are asking if I can "just bill insurance for them."
Solution: "I appreciate you asking, but I'm no longer credentialed with insurance companies, which means I legally cannot bill them. I can provide you with a superbill to submit yourself if you have out-of-network benefits."

(Do NOT bill insurance once you've terminated. That's fraud.)

Problem: I'm lonely and miss having colleagues.
Solution:
- Join a consultation group (peer or paid)
- Co-work with other therapists (virtual or in-person)
- Join online communities (Private Pay Practitioners Facebook group)
- Attend local professional events

- Schedule regular coffee meetings with other therapists

Loneliness is the #1 unexpected challenge of private pay. Plan for it.

Problem: A former client is upset about the transition and badmouthing me online.
Solution:
- Do not engage publicly or respond to reviews
- Document everything (save messages, reviews)
- Consult with a healthcare attorney if needed
- Focus on providing excellent care to current clients (good reviews will outweigh bad ones)
- Remember: You can't please everyone, and that's okay

Problem: I'm second-guessing my decision and want to go back to insurance.
Solution:
- Wait. Give it the full 90 days before making any decisions.
- Review your original reasons for leaving (go back to Chapter 1)
- Look at your actual numbers, not your feelings
- Talk to other private pay therapists who've been through this
- Ask yourself: What would need to change to make this work?

Most panic happens in weeks 2-6. Push through.

Problem: Insurance is still sending me claims or trying to enroll me.
Solution:
- Double-check that your termination was properly processed
- Call provider relations and confirm your termination date
- Update your CAQH profile to "inactive"
- Keep documentation of all termination correspondence
- If they continue to send claims, return them with a note: "Provider terminated from panel effective [date]"

Problem: My practice is filling up too fast.
Solution: Good problem to have! Now you get to be selective.
- Raise your rates (you're in demand)
- Create a waitlist
- Consider starting a group or intensive to serve more people
- Focus on your ideal clients only
- Build systems to manage high volume

THIS IS TEMPORARY:

Whatever problem you're facing in the transition, it's temporary.

Give yourself 90 days of consistent effort before evaluating.

Most therapists who successfully transition report that months 4-6 are when things really click.

You've got this.

NEXT SECTION: Chapter 2 - Know Your Why & Your Who

Chapter 2

Know Your Why & Your Who

You can't build a sustainable practice without two things:
1. A clear reason WHY you're doing this
2. A specific understanding of WHO you serve

This isn't theoretical. This is the foundation of everything else.

Your "why" keeps you going when it's hard. Your "who" determines your marketing, your messaging, and your success.

Get these right, and everything else gets easier.

Reference: Chapter 2 in the Private Pay Practitioners Playbook

TIME TO COMPLETE: 2-3 hours

Let's start with your why.

YOUR WHY STATEMENT
Why This Work Matters to You

Your why isn't about money. Money is a result, not a reason.
Your why is deeper. It's personal. It's what keeps you showing up.

Answer these questions:

1. Why did you become a therapist in the first place?
_____
_____
_____
_____

2. What life experiences shaped your decision to do this work?
_____
_____
_____
_____
_____
_____
_____
_____

3. What change do you want to create in the world through your work?
_____
_____
_____
_____
_____
_____
_____

4. When you think about your ideal practice, what does it allow you to do? (For your clients? For yourself? For your life?)
_____
_____
_____
_____

5. What would make you feel like your practice was successful (beyond income)?

_____
_____
_____
_____
_____
_____
_____

Now distill all of that into one statement:

YOUR WHY STATEMENT:
I do this work because

_____
_____
_____
_____
_____
_____
_____
_____

This matters to me because

_____
_____
_____
_____
_____
_____
_____
_____

When my practice is successful, it means

_____
_____

_____
_____
_____
_____
_____

Read this statement when:
- You're questioning your rates
- You're scared to market yourself
- A potential client says no
- You're feeling burned out
- You forget why you started

This is your anchor. Keep it visible.

IDEAL CLIENT AVATAR

Get SPECIFIC About Who You Serve

"I help everyone" = You help no one.

Your ideal client is a specific person with specific problems.
The more specific you get, the easier marketing becomes.

PART 1: DEMOGRAPHICS
- Age range: _____
- Gender: _____
- Relationship status: _____
- Do they have kids? ☐ Yes ☐ No ☐ Either
- Career/profession: _____
- Income level: ☐ $50-75k ☐ $75-100k ☐ $100-150k ☐ $150k+
- Education level: _____
- Location: _____

PART 2: PSYCHOGRAPHICS (This is what really matters)

What do they value most in life?

___

What are they struggling with right now? (Be specific)

___

What have they already tried to fix this problem?

___

What's keeping them stuck?

___

What do they believe about themselves that's holding them back?
___

What do they want their life to look like?
___

What are they afraid will happen if nothing changes?
___

PART 3: THERAPY-SPECIFIC QUESTIONS

What brings them to therapy NOW? (What's the trigger?)
___

Have they been to therapy before?
- Yes
- No
- Mixed

If yes, what was their experience?

What are they skeptical about when it comes to therapy?

What do they need from a therapist?

What do they NOT want from a therapist?

_____
_____
_____
_____
_____
_____
_____

PART 4: PAIN POINTS & DESIRES

What keeps them up at night?

_____
_____
_____
_____
_____
_____
_____

What do they complain about to friends?

_____
_____
_____
_____
_____
_____
_____

What would make them say "YES! This therapist gets me!"?

_____
_____
_____
_____

What transformation are they looking for?
FROM: _____

TO: _____

PART 5: CREATE A SPECIFIC PERSON

Give them a name: _____
Describe a day in their life:

What would they Google when looking for a therapi
_____
_____
_____
_____
_____
_____
_____
_____

What would make them choose YOU over another therapist?
_____
_____
_____
_____
_____
_____
_____
_____

YOUR IDEAL CLIENT SUMMARY:
My ideal client is a _____-year-old _____ who struggles with
_____
_____
_____
_____

They come to therapy because
_____
_____
_____

They value _____
_____
_____

They're looking for a therapist who
_____
_____

I'm the right fit for them because
_____
_____
_____
_____
_____

REALITY CHECK:

Can this person afford your private pay rate?
- Yes
- No
- Maybe

If no or maybe, you need to adjust either your rate or your ideal client.

Are there enough of these people in your area?
- Yes
- No
- Maybe

If no, you need to either expand your reach (telehealth) or adjust your niche.

Do you actually ENJOY working with this person?
- Yes
- No

If no, start over. Don't build a practice around people you don't want to work with.

NICHE DISCOVERY
What Makes *YOU* Different?

Your niche isn't just about who you serve. It's about what YOU bring to the table.

YOUR EXPERIENCE & EXPERTISE
What personal experiences inform your work?
_____
_____
_____
_____
_____
_____
_____
_____

What professional experiences make you qualified?
_____
_____
_____
_____
_____
_____
_____

What specialized training or certifications do you have?
_____
_____
_____
_____
_____
_____
_____

What do clients consistently say you're good at?
_____
_____
_____
_____
_____
_____
_____

What types of cases do you find most fulfilling?
_____
_____
_____
_____
_____
_____
_____

What do other therapists refer to you for?
_____
_____
_____
_____
_____
_____
_____

YOUR UNIQUE PERSPECTIVE
How is your approach different from other therapists?
_____
_____
_____
_____
_____

What do you believe about therapy that not everyone agrees with?
_____
_____
_____
_____
_____
_____
_____

What's your philosophy about change/healing/growth?
_____
_____
_____
_____
_____
_____
_____

YOUR NICHE STATEMENT:

I specialize in helping
_____
_____ (specific type of person)

who struggle with
_____
_____ (specific problem)

My approach is unique because
_____
_____

I'm the right fit for people who want

___

TEST YOUR NICHE:

Is it specific enough that you can explain it in one sentence?
- Yes
- No

Does it attract your ideal clients?
- Yes
- No
- Not sure yet

Does it repel people who aren't a good fit?
- Yes
- No

(If it doesn't repel anyone, it's not specific enough)

Do you feel confident claiming this expertise?
- Yes
- No

If you answered no to any of these, refine your niche statement.

___

VOICE & POSITIONING

How You Talk About What You Do

Your voice is how you communicate. Your positioning is how you're perceived.

Both matter.

___

YOUR COMMUNICATION STYLE

How do you naturally talk to clients? (Check all that apply)
- Warm and nurturing
- Direct and straightforward
- Humorous and lighthearted
- Professional and polished
- Casual and conversational
- Challenging and provocative
- Calm and steady
- Energetic and enthusiastic

What words describe how you want clients to feel when they read your website or talk to you?
_____
_____
_____
_____
_____
_____
_____
_____

What words describe how you DON'T want to come across?
_____
_____
_____
_____
_____
_____
_____

YOUR POSITIONING

How do you want to be perceived in the marketplace?
- The expert/specialist (high credibility, premium positioning)
- The guide/mentor (supportive, experienced, trustworthy)
- The challenger (pushes people, direct, results-focused)
- The healer (holistic, integrative, transformational)
- The ally/advocate (social justice-focused, community-oriented)
- Other: _____

YOUR PROFESSIONAL BIO (First Draft)

Write 3-4 sentences about yourself in your natural voice:
Who you are, what you do, who you help, what makes you different.

_____
_____
_____
_____
_____
_____
_____
_____
_____
_____
_____
_____
_____
_____
_____
_____
_____
_____
_____

Read it out loud. Does it sound like YOU?
- Yes
- No

If no, rewrite it until it does.

YOUR ELEVATOR PITCH

You have 30 seconds to tell someone what you do. What do you say?

_____
_____
_____
_____
_____
_____
_____
_____
_____
_____
_____
_____
_____
_____
_____
_____
_____
_____
_____

Practice this until it rolls off your tongue naturally.

_____

POSITIONING STATEMENT:
I'm a
_____
_____ who helps
_____
_____ (your role) (specific people)
with
_____

_____
_____(specific problem)

My approach is
_____
_____
_____

I'm the right therapist for people who
_____
_____
_____
_____

This becomes the foundation of your website, social media, and networking conversations.

PRACTICE VALUES

What Matters Most in How You Work

Your values determine your policies, your boundaries, and your decision-making.
Get clear on them now.

CORE VALUES EXERCISE

Circle the 5 values that matter most to you in your practice:

Autonomy Flexibility Connection Quality Growth Impact Integrity Authenticity Efficiency
Sustainability Innovation Accessibility Excellence Balance Community Respect Creativity
Simplicity Justice Freedom Stability

Your top 5:
1. _____
2. _____

3. _____
4. _____
5. _____

_____

For each value, answer:

VALUE 1: _____

What does this look like in your practice?

_____
_____
_____
_____

How does this influence your policies or decisions?

_____
_____
_____
_____

VALUE 2: _____

What does this look like in your practice?

_____
_____
_____
_____

How does this influence your policies or decisions?

_____
_____
_____
_____

VALUE 3: _____

What does this look like in your practice?

How does this influence your policies or decisions?

VALUE 4: _____

What does this look like in your practice?

How does this influence your policies or decisions?

VALUE 5: _____

What does this look like in your practice?

How does this influence your policies or decisions?

VALUES-BASED DECISIONS:

When you're making a difficult decision about your practice, ask:

"Does this align with my core values?"

If no, don't do it.

Examples:
- Should I offer a sliding scale? (Does it align with accessibility vs. sustainability?)
- Should I respond to emails at 9pm? (Does it align with boundaries vs. client service?)
- Should I take this client who's not my ideal fit? (Does it align with integrity vs. income needs?)

Your values are your compass.

Chapter 2: Action Items

CHAPTER 2: WHAT YOU'VE CREATED
- Your Why Statement
- Your Ideal Client Avatar
- Your Niche Statement
- Your Voice & Positioning
- Your Core Values

This is your foundation. Everything else builds from here.

IMMEDIATE ACTION ITEMS:
- Save your why statement somewhere visible (phone wallpaper, office wall)
- Share your ideal client description with 3 people and ask: "Does this make sense? Can you picture this person?"
- Practice your elevator pitch with someone this week
- Review your current website/social media: Does it speak to your ideal client? If no, make a list of what needs to change.
- Make one decision this week based on your core values (what will you say yes or no to?)

REFLECTION:

What surprised you most about this chapter?

_____
_____
_____
_____
_____
_____
_____
_____
_____
_____
_____
_____

What feels most clear now?
_____
_____
_____
_____
_____
_____
_____

What still feels uncertain?
_____
_____
_____
_____
_____
_____
_____
_____

NEXT: Chapter 3 - Messaging That Converts
Now that you know WHY you do this and WHO you serve, let's talk about HOW to communicate it.
_____

Chapter 3

Messaging That Converts

You know who you serve. Now you need to tell them.

But here's the problem: Most therapist websites and marketing sound exactly the same. "I provide a safe, non-judgmental space..." "I use evidence-based approaches..." "I work with adults experiencing anxiety, depression, and life transitions..." Your ideal clients scroll right past that. This chapter helps you create messaging that makes people stop and say, "This therapist gets me."

You'll create:
- Website copy that speaks directly to your ideal client
- Headlines that grab attention
- Your story in a way that connects
- Social media content that feels authentic
- Boundary language that protects your time

Reference: Chapter 3 in the Private Pay Practitioners Playbook
TIME TO COMPLETE: 2-3 hours

Let's start with your website.

WEBSITE MESSAGING AUDIT

Does Your Current Site Speak to Your Ideal Client?

Go to your website (or imagine what it will say if you don't have one yet).

Answer honestly:

_____

HOME PAGE:

Does your headline immediately tell people who you help and what problem you solve?
- Yes
- No
- Sort of
- Don't have a website yet

Can someone understand what you do within 5 seconds of landing on your site?
- Yes
- No
- Sort of

Does your homepage speak directly to your ideal client's pain points?
- Yes
- No
- Sort of

Is your call-to-action clear? (What do you want them to do next?)
- Yes
- No
- Sort of

ABOUT PAGE:

Does your bio explain why you do this work, not just your credentials?
- Yes
- No
- Sort of
- Don't have an about page

Does it connect your personal experience to why you're qualified to help them?
- Yes
- No
- Sort of

Does it sound like YOU, or does it sound like every other therapist?
- Sounds like me
- Sounds generic

SERVICES PAGE:
Do you clearly explain what working with you looks like?
- Yes
- No
- Sort of
- Don't have a services page

Do you list your rate without making people dig for it?
- Yes
- No
- It's there but buried

Do you explain what makes your approach different?
- Yes
- No
- Sort of

CONTACT/SCHEDULING:
Is it easy to schedule a consultation or contact you?
- Very easy
- Somewhat easy
- Confusing
- Not set up yet

Do you have a clear intake process explained?
- Yes
- No
- Sort of

OVERALL IMPRESSION:
If your ideal client landed on your site, would they feel like you understand them?
- Definitely
- Probably
- Probably not
- Definitely not

Does your website differentiate you from other therapists?
- Yes, clearly
- Somewhat
- No, I sound like everyone else

WHAT NEEDS TO CHANGE:
Based on this audit, list 3-5 things you need to update:

1. _____
2. _____
3. _____
4. _____
5. _____

Priority order: Which one will you tackle first? _____

HEADLINE FORMULA WORKSHEET

Write 10 Different Headlines for Your Practice

Your headline is the first thing people see. It needs to do two things:
1. Tell them WHO you help
2. Tell them WHAT you help with

Use these formulas to create options. Write at least 10. Pick your favorite.

FORMULA 1: "I help [specific people] [achieve specific outcome]"
Example: "I help high-achieving professionals overcome burnout and rediscover meaning in their work"

Your version:
_____
_____
_____
_____

FORMULA 2: "[Specific problem]? [Specific solution]."
Example: "Stuck in cycles of relationship anxiety? Let's break the pattern."

Your version:
_____
_____
_____
_____

FORMULA 3: "Therapy for [specific people] who [specific situation]"
Example: "Therapy for parents who feel like they're failing (you're not)"

Your version:
_____
_____
_____
_____

FORMULA 4: "[Outcome] without [thing they're worried about]"
Example: "Heal from trauma without reliving every painful detail"

Your version:
_____
_____
_____
_____

FORMULA 5: "You don't have to [struggle]. [Solution exists]."
Example: "You don't have to white-knuckle your sobriety. There's a better way."
Your version:
_____
_____
_____
_____

FORMULA 6: "[Empathy statement]. [What you offer]."
Example: "Sex addiction is isolating. You don't have to figure this out alone."

Your version:

FORMULA 7: "Ready to [desired outcome]? Start here."
Example: "Ready to stop people-pleasing and set actual boundaries? Start here."

Your version:
_____
_____
_____
_____

FORMULA 8: "[Question your ideal client asks]. Here's how."
Example: "Can I really change my relationship with food? Here's how."

Your version:
_____
_____
_____
_____

FORMULA 9: "[Specific niche] therapy that actually [outcome]"
Example: "EMDR therapy that actually helps you move forward, not just talk about the past"

Your version:
_____
_____
_____
_____

FORMULA 10: Free write your own
_____
_____
_____
_____

Now pick your top 3 and test them:
1. _____
2. _____
3. _____

Show these to 3 people (ideally people who fit your ideal client profile) and ask: "Which one makes you most curious? Which one makes you feel understood?"

Their feedback:

_____
_____
_____
_____
_____
_____
_____
_____

Your final headline choice:

_____
_____
_____
_____
_____

YOUR STORY TEMPLATE

Connect Through Your Experience

People connect with stories, not credentials.

Your About page should tell your story in a way that builds trust and shows why you're qualified to help.

Use this template:

_____

PARAGRAPH 1: THE HOOK (Why you do this work)

Start with something that connects to your ideal client's experience or your personal why. Example: "I became a therapist because I know what it's like to feel stuck. For years, I..."

Your version:
_____
_____
_____
_____
_____
_____

PARAGRAPH 2: YOUR JOURNEY (How you got here)

Share the relevant parts of your story that show you understand what they're going through. Example: "After my own experience with [relevant struggle], I realized that [insight]. That's what led me to specialize in [your niche]."

Your version:
_____
_____
_____
_____
_____
_____

PARAGRAPH 3: YOUR APPROACH (How you work)

Explain your philosophy and what makes your approach different.

Example: "I don't believe therapy has to take years to work. My approach combines [methods] with [what makes you different]. We focus on [your focus]."

Your version:
_____
_____
_____

PARAGRAPH 4: WHO YOU WORK WITH (Your ideal client)

Be specific about who you help and what you help them with.

Example: "I work with [specific people] who are struggling with [specific issue]. My clients are typically [description] who want [outcome]."

Your version:

___

PARAGRAPH 5: THE INVITATION (Call to action)

Tell them what to do next.

Example: "If this resonates with you, I'd love to talk. Schedule a free consultation to see if we're a good fit."

Your version:

___

Now put it all together and read it out loud.

Does it sound like you?
- Yes
- No

Does it connect your story to their experience?
- Yes
- No

Does it differentiate you from other therapists?
- Yes
- No

If you answered no to any of these, revise until all three are yes.

30-DAY SOCIAL MEDIA CONTENT PLANNER

What to Post When You Don't Know What to Post

Consistent posting builds visibility. But you don't need to post every day. Aim for 3-4 posts per week. Use this guide to plan a month of content.

CONTENT CATEGORIES (Rotate through these):

1. **EDUCATIONAL**: Teach something relevant to your niche
2. **PERSONAL**: Share something about you (builds connection)
3. **PROFESSIONAL INSIGHT**: Share a clinical insight, concept, or professional observation
4. **MYTH-BUSTING**: Challenge a common misconception
5. **BEHIND-THE-SCENES**: How you work, your process
6. **ENGAGEMENT**: Ask a question, start a conversation
7. **PROMOTIONAL**: You have openings, you're accepting new clients

WEEK 1 POSTS:

POST 1 (Educational):
- Topic: _____
- Key point: _____
- Call to action: _____

POST 2 (Personal):
- What I'll share: _____
- Why it matters to my ideal client: _____

POST 3 (Myth-Busting):
- Myth: _____
- Truth: _____
- Why this matters: _____

_____

WEEK 2 POSTS:

POST 1 (Behind-the-Scenes):
- What I'll show: _____
- What they'll learn: _____

POST 2 (Educational):
- Topic: _____
- Key point: _____
- Call to action: _____

POST 3 (Engagement):
- Question I'll ask: _____
- Why this matters to my niche: _____

_____

WEEK 3 POSTS:

POST 1 (Professional Insight):
- What's one thing you've learned recently in your practice? A clinical concept, research finding, or observation about your specialty:

  _____
  _____
  _____

- Why this matters to your ideal client:

  _____
  _____
  _____
  _____

POST 2 (Personal):
- What I'll share:

  _____
  _____
  _____

- Connection to my work:

  _____
  _____
  _____

POST 3 (Educational):
- Topic:

  _____
  _____
  _____

- Key point:

  _____
  _____
  _____

- Call to action:

  _____
  _____
  _____

WEEK 4 POSTS:

POST 1 (Myth-Busting):
- Myth:
  _____
  _____

- Truth:
  _____
  _____

- Why this matters:
  _____
  _____
  _____

POST 2 (Promotional):
- What I'm offering:
  _____
  _____

- Who it's for:
  _____
  _____
  _____

- How to get started:
  _____
  _____
  _____

POST 3 (Engagement):
1. Question I'll ask:
   _____
   _____

2. Why this matters to my niche:
   _____
   _____
   _____

CONTENT SWIPE FILE
Keep a running list of post ideas so you never run out:

EDUCATIONAL TOPICS (Things your ideal client needs to know):
1. _____
2. _____
3. _____
4. _____
5. _____

MYTHS TO BUST (Things your ideal client believes that aren't true):
1. _____
2. _____
3. _____

ENGAGEMENT QUESTIONS (Things that will get your ideal client talking):
1. _____
2. _____
3. _____

PERSONAL STORIES (Things about you that build connection):
1. _____
2. _____
3. _____

CONTENT GUIDELINES:

- Every post should relate to your niche somehow
- Every post should speak directly to your ideal client
- Don't use therapy jargon (write like you talk)
- Include a clear next step (DM me, schedule a call, save this post)
- Use line breaks for readability
- Don't over-hashtag (5-10 max, use relevant ones)

PLATFORMS:

Which platform(s) will you focus on? (Pick 1-2 max)
- Instagram

- Facebook
- LinkedIn
- TikTok
- Threads
- Other: _____

Don't try to be everywhere. Master one platform first.

BATCH CONTENT CREATION:

Schedule 2 hours once a week to:
1. Write all your posts for the week
2. Create any graphics (Canva)
3. Schedule them (Later, Buffer, or native scheduling)

Batch day/time: _____

This is more efficient than posting in the moment.

BOUNDARY LANGUAGE SCRIPTS
How to Communicate Policies Clearly

Your boundaries protect your practice. But you need to communicate them clearly. Here's the language:

CANCELLATION POLICY

"I require 24 hours' notice for cancellations. Late cancellations or no-shows are charged the full session fee. This policy allows me to offer your time to someone else on my waitlist and keeps my practice sustainable."

Your version:
_____
_____
_____
_____

AFTER-HOURS CONTACT

"I check email once per day during business hours (9am-5pm, Monday-Friday). If you're experiencing a mental health emergency, please call 988 or go to your nearest emergency room. I'm not able to provide crisis support via email or text."

Your version:
_____
_____
_____
_____
_____
_____
_____
_____

SESSION LENGTH

"Sessions are 50 minutes. We'll end on time even if you arrive late. This allows me to stay on schedule for other clients and maintain consistent boundaries."

Your version:
_____
_____
_____
_____
_____
_____
_____
_____

PAYMENT POLICY

"Payment is due at the time of service. I accept [payment methods]. If your card is declined, I'll reach out before your next session to update payment information."

Your version:

_____
_____
_____
_____
_____
_____
_____
_____

SCOPE OF SERVICES

"I provide outpatient therapy for [your niche]. I don't provide court evaluations, disability assessments, or letters for ESA animals. If you need these services, I can refer you to appropriate providers."

Your version:

_____
_____
_____
_____
_____
_____
_____
_____

COMMUNICATION BETWEEN SESSIONS

"Brief check-ins between sessions are fine via [email/portal]. For longer conversations or crisis support, we'll need to schedule a session. I typically respond to messages within 24-48 business hours."

Your version:

_____
_____
_____
_____
_____
_____
_____

THE KEY TO BOUNDARIES:

State them clearly. Don't apologize. Don't over-explain.

"This is my policy" is a complete sentence.

Your policies protect your practice. Communicate them with confidence.

___

Chapter 4

The Client Journey

Why This Chapter Matters

You can be the best therapist in the world, but if your client journey feels confusing, impersonal, or inconsistent, people won't stick around long enough to experience your clinical brilliance.

Think about it: Your client's experience starts way before they sit down for their first session. It begins the moment they find your website. It continues through every email, every phone interaction, every detail of how you run your practice.

Here's what I've learned after years of building my practice and consulting with hundreds of therapists: **the difference between practices that struggle with retention and those with waiting lists often comes down to the client experience, not clinical skill.**

This chapter is about mapping out every touchpoint in your client's journey and making each one intentional. We're going to cover all seven stages:
- Discovery (how they find you)
- First Contact (their initial impression)
- Consultation (if you do them)
- Onboarding (between "yes" and session one)
- First Session (setting the tone)
- Ongoing Sessions (the work itself)
- Ending/Transition (how you close well)

Great messaging gets people in the door. A great client experience keeps them there and turns them into your biggest referral sources.

Let's build yours.

___

Your Complete Client Journey Map

Instructions: Map out each stage of YOUR current client journey. Be honest about what's actually happening, not what you wish was happening. We'll identify gaps and opportunities as we go.

Stage 1: Discovery

How do potential clients find you?
- Google search
- Psychology Today
- Therapy directories (which ones?): _____
- Referrals from other professionals
- Word of mouth from current/former clients
- Social media (which platforms?): _____
- Other: _____

What's the first thing they see when they find you?
My website homepage message says:

_____
_____
_____
_____
_____
_____
_____
_____

Time spent on your website before contacting you: Most people spend 4-5 minutes deciding if you're the right fit. What are they reading during that time?

Content they're reading:
- About page (does it show your personality?)
- Services page (does it speak to their struggles?)
- FAQ page (does it answer their real questions?)
- Blog/resources (are they current?)
- Contact page (is it easy to take the next step?)

First Impression Audit:

Rate each element honestly (1=needs work, 5=excellent):

Element	Rating	What needs to improve?
Website photos show warmth and personality	___/5	
Language speaks to internal experience, not just symptoms	___/5	
Clear next steps for contacting you	___/5	
Mobile-friendly and easy to navigate	___/5	
Loads quickly without technical issues	___/5	

Stage 2: First Contact and Prequalifying

How do people currently reach out to you?
- Phone call
- Email through website
- Contact form
- Text message
- Social media DM
- Scheduling link directly

Your response time: I typically respond within: _____ (be honest!)

Your prequalifying process (or lack thereof):
Do you currently prequalify potential clients?
- Yes
- No
- Sort of

If yes, how?

_____
_____
_____
_____
_____
_____

Prequalifying Questions Framework

These questions help ideal clients self-select, saving you time on consultations that won't convert.

Question 1: Motivation and Timing "What led you to seek therapy right now?"

This tells you: _____
_____
_____
_____

Question 2: Previous Experience "Have you worked with a therapist before? If so, what was helpful or unhelpful about that experience?"

This reveals: _____
_____
_____
_____

Question 3: Goals and Readiness "What are your goals for therapy? What do you hope will be different in 3-6 months?"

Vague answers might mean: _____
_____
_____
_____

Question 4: Private Pay Understanding "Are you familiar with how private pay therapy works?"

This assesses: _____
_____
_____
_____

Question 5: Commitment Level "How do you plan to prioritize the time and financial investment in this work?"

This tells you: _____
_____
_____
_____

Private Pay Practitioners Workbook

Red Flags Checklist

Check any that are current issues in your practice:
- People asking about insurance when your website clearly states you don't bill
- Rate shopping or trying to negotiate your fees
- Wanting a "quick fix" or unclear about therapy goals
- Unwillingness to commit to regular sessions
- Expecting you to solve problems they're not willing to work on
- Extensive back-and-forth emails before scheduling

Your Red Flags:

Based on your experience, what are YOUR specific red flags?
1. _____
2. _____
3. _____

_____

Stage 3: The Consultation Decision Point

Do you offer consultation calls?
- Yes
- No
- Thinking about it

If YES, continue here. If NO, skip to Stage 4.

Your Consultation Call Script Builder

Opening (First 2 minutes)

"Hi [Name], thanks for scheduling this consultation! I have about [TIME] to talk today. Before we dive in, can you tell me..."

Finish this opener in your own words:

_____
_____
_____
_____
_____
_____

Private Pay Practitioners Workbook

Core Questions (10-12 minutes)

Question 1 about their current situation:
_____
_____
_____
_____

Question 2 about their goals:
_____
_____
_____
_____

Question 3 about readiness/commitment:
_____
_____
_____
_____

Explaining Your Approach (3-4 minutes)

"Based on what you're sharing, it sounds like [SUMMARIZE THEIR CONCERNS]. I work with a lot of people who are experiencing similar challenges."

My approach in plain language (no jargon):
_____
_____
_____
_____
_____
_____

What I find most effective is:
_____
_____
_____
_____
_____
_____

Discussing Fees and Logistics (2-3 minutes)

My exact language for explaining fees:
"My fee is $_____ per session. Sessions are _____ minutes.

I require _____ notice for cancellations.

Payment is _____ _____ (at each session/monthly/etc.)

I don't bill insurance, but I can provide a superbill for you to submit for out-of-network reimbursement."

Closing the Consultation (2-3 minutes)

If they seem like a good fit:

"It sounds like we might be a good fit. Here's what happens next..."

_____
_____
_____
_____
_____
_____
_____

If they're NOT a good fit:
"Based on what you've shared, I think you might be better served by..."

_____
_____
_____
_____
_____
_____
_____

If they need time to think:
"Take your time thinking it over. If you'd like to move forward..."

_____
_____
_____
_____
_____
_____
_____

OR: The Streamlined Approach (My Method)

If you DON'T do consultation calls, how do you handle initial contact?

Clear website information I provide upfront:
- Who I work with specifically
- What my approach involves
- What my fees are
- How the process works
- What to expect in first session

Phone call protocol:
If someone calls, I will answer quick questions for _____ minutes maximum.

I will NOT: _____

I direct them to: _____

Email protocol:
I answer brief questions like:
_____
_____
_____
_____

I don't engage in:
_____
_____
_____
_____

After _____ emails back and forth, I suggest:
_____
_____
_____
_____
_____

Stage 4: Onboarding Checklist

Between "yes" and the first session, what happens?

Your Confirmation Email Template

Subject line: _____

Hi [Name],

Great! I'm looking forward to working together.

Your first appointment is:
Date: _____
Time: _____
Location/Platform: _____

Before our first session:
- What they need to do
- What paperwork to complete
- What to expect

My cancellation policy:
_____
_____
_____
_____

Payment information:
_____
_____
_____
_____

If you have any questions before we meet, feel free to reach out.

[Your signature]

Pre-Session Preparation

What do clients need to complete before session one?
- Intake paperwork (how do they access it?): _____
- HIPAA consent forms
- Payment information
- Insurance superbill information (if applicable)
- Background questionnaire
- Goal-setting worksheet
- Other: _____

How far in advance do you send this? _____

Follow-up: Do you send a reminder?
- Yes
- No

If yes, when? _____

Stage 5: The First Session Framework

Your First Session Structure

Time: _____ minutes total

Part 1: Welcome and Orientation (____ min)
Opening words:
_____
_____
_____

Part 2: Why Now? (____ min)
"Tell me what's bringing you in right now. What made this the right time?"
Why this matters: This reinforces their motivation and commitment

Part 3: Goals and Expectations (____ min)
Questions I ask about their goals:
1. _____
2. _____
3. _____

Part 4: Explaining Your Approach (_____ min)
How I explain my therapeutic approach in plain language:

_____
_____
_____
_____

Part 5: Setting the Framework (_____ min)
I set expectations about:
- How often we'll meet (my recommendation: _____)
- What they can expect from me (I will: _____)
- What I need from them (Please: _____)
- How we'll track progress (We'll: _____)
- What success looks like (You'll notice: _____)

Part 6: Beginning the Work (_____ min)
First therapeutic intervention or exercise:

_____
_____
_____
_____
_____
_____
_____
_____

Part 7: Closing (_____ min)
Before they leave, I always:
- Schedule the next appointment
- Give them something to think about or work on
- Reiterate one thing from our session
- Remind them how to reach me between sessions
- Other: _____

Stage 6: Ongoing Sessions Experience
Creating Consistency and Value

Your Reliable Structure

Session timing:
- Same day/time each week (preferred)
- Flexible scheduling
- Rotating schedule

Session format:
- 50 minutes
- 60 minutes
- 90 minutes
- Other: _____

How I handle schedule changes:
_____
_____
_____
_____

Demonstrating Value Throughout

Progress check-ins: How often do you explicitly discuss progress with clients?
- Every session
- Monthly
- Every 3 months
- When they bring it up
- Honestly? Not enough

Between-session support: What do you offer between sessions?
- Homework/exercises
- Resources/articles
- Email check-ins (how often?: _____)
- Text reminders
- Nothing currently
- Other: _____

Celebrating progress: How do you acknowledge growth?
_____
_____
_____
_____

Building the Relationship

What helps you remember session details?
- Notes system: _____
- Post-session reflection: _____
- Session recording (with consent): _____

How do you show genuine curiosity?
_____
_____
_____
_____

How do you maintain boundaries while being present?
_____
_____
_____
_____
_____

Stage 7: Endings and Transitions
Planning for Different Types of Endings

When Therapy Goals Are Met

My planned termination process:
Number of "termination" sessions: _____

What I cover in these sessions:
- Acknowledge progress made
- Reinforce their growth and capabilities
- Discuss maintenance of changes
- Leave the door open for future check-ins
- Ask for feedback about their experience
- Request a testimonial/review (if appropriate)

My exact language for initiating termination:

"It seems like you've made real progress on _____.

Let's talk about whether it makes sense to start thinking about wrapping up our work together..."

When a Referral Is Needed

Situations where I refer out:
1. _____
2. _____
3. _____

How I handle referrals:
My approach:
- Be honest about when someone needs different expertise
- Provide specific, warm referrals (not just names)
- Offer to communicate with the new provider (with permission)
- Frame the referral as continued care, not rejection
- Follow up to ensure they connected

My referral language:
"I've been thinking about what you shared, and I believe you would benefit from..."
_____
_____
_____
_____

My referral list:

Specialty Needed	Provider Name	Contact Info	Why I Trust Them

When Clients Choose to End

If a client wants to stop, I:
- Respect their decision while offering to discuss concerns
- Provide a summary of progress made
- Offer resources for continued growth
- Maintain warmth and professionalism
- Leave the door open for returning

My response when someone wants to end:
"I appreciate you being direct with me. Can we take one session to talk about your experience and wrap things up well?"

_____
_____
_____
_____

The Ghosting Protocol
What I do when a client disappears:
After _____ missed sessions with no contact, I:
Week 1: _____
Week 2: _____
Week 3: _____
Week 4: _____

My "checking in" message template:
_____
_____
_____
_____

When I close a file:
After _____ weeks/months of no contact, I:
- Send a final email
- Close their file
- Note in my records
- Keep the door open for future contact

Your Complete Client Journey Map

Now put it all together:

Draw your complete journey from discovery to ending. Include approximate timeframes for each stage.

DISCOVERY → [____ days/weeks] → **FIRST CONTACT** → [____ hours/days] →

CONSULTATION/SCREENING → [____ days] → **ONBOARDING** → [____ days] →

FIRST SESSION → [ongoing] → **REGULAR SESSIONS** → [varies] → **ENDING**

Where do people drop out in your current process?
1. _____
2. _____
3. _____

What touchpoints could you improve to demonstrate value better?
1. _____
2. _____
3. _____

What feedback have you received about your process that you haven't acted on?
_____
_____
_____
_____
_____

Chapter 4 Action Items

Do these BEFORE moving to the next chapter:
- Immediate: Map your current client journey using the framework above
- This week: Identify the ONE place where your process feels weakest or where clients get confused
- This week: Create or update your consultation call script (if you use consultations)
- This week: Write your confirmation email template for new clients
- This month: Design your complete onboarding process with specific timelines
- This month: Create your referral list with at least 5 trusted providers
- This month: Test your first session structure with the next new client
- Ongoing: Track where potential clients drop out of your process for the next 30 days

---

Reflection Questions

Take 10 minutes to think through these:

1. Where in your current process do potential clients get confused or drop out?

   _____
   _____
   _____
   _____
   _____

2. What would make your client experience feel more intentional and cohesive?

   _____
   _____
   _____
   _____
   _____

3. If you were a potential client, what would make you choose you over another therapist with similar credentials?

   _____
   _____
   _____
   _____
   _____

4. **What's the difference between how you want your client experience to feel and how it actually feels right now?**

   _____
   _____
   _____
   _____
   _____

5. **What's ONE thing you can improve THIS WEEK that would make the biggest difference?**

   _____
   _____
   _____
   _____
   _____

Remember

Creating an experience rather than just offering sessions is what transforms a practice from transactional to transformational.

Your clinical skills make you a good therapist. Your client journey makes you a successful practice owner.

Every touchpoint matters. Every email, every phone call, every transition between stages shapes how clients perceive the value of working with you.

The practices that thrive aren't necessarily run by the most clinically gifted therapists. They're run by therapists who understand that building a sustainable private pay practice requires attention to the entire client experience, not just what happens in the therapy room.

Now go build a client journey that matches the quality of your clinical work.

End of Chapter 4 | Continue to Chapter 5: Networking That Actually Works

Chapter 5

Networking That Actually Works

Beyond the Business Cards

Let's be real: most therapists hate networking. It feels sales-y, fake, and exhausting. But here's the truth: networking for therapists isn't about working a room or collecting business cards. It's about building genuine professional relationships with people who serve similar clients.

The practitioners who fill their practices aren't the ones with the slickest elevator pitch. They're the ones who show up consistently, add value first, and build real relationships over time. This chapter gives you the exact systems and scripts to network without feeling gross about it.

The Coffee Chat Framework

How to Have Productive Networking Conversations

Coffee chats (virtual or in-person) are one of the most effective networking tools for private pay practitioners. Here's how to make them work:

Before the Chat:
Research their practice
- Look at their website and social media
- Note their specialties and ideal clients
- Identify potential overlap or complementary niches

Set a clear intention: What do you want from this connection?
- Learn about their practice model?
- Explore potential referral partnerships?
- Get advice on a specific challenge?

Prepare 3-5 questions

Write your questions here:
1. _____
2. _____
3. _____
4. _____
5. _____

During the Chat:

The Opening (5 minutes) Start with genuine connection:
- "Thanks for making time to connect. I've been following your work with [specialty] and wanted to learn more about your practice."
- Keep it conversational, not scripted

The Middle (20-30 minutes) Be interested, not just interesting:
- Ask about their journey into private practice
- Learn about their ideal clients and specialties
- Ask: "What kind of referrals are you looking for right now?"
- Share about your practice authentically

The Close (5 minutes) End with clarity:
- "I'd love to stay connected. What's the best way to refer clients to you?"
- "Can I add you to my referral list?"
- Offer value: "I'd be happy to connect you with [specific person/resource]."

After the Chat (Within 24 Hours):
- Send thank you note (see template on page 65)
- Connect on LinkedIn or other business social media platforms
- Follow through on anything you promised
- Add them to your referral network tracker

REFERRAL TRACKING WORKSHEET

Your Professional Network at a Glance

Use this tracker to organize your referral sources and stay on top of follow-ups.

Contact Name	Specialty / Focus	Last Contact	Referrals Given	Referrals Received	Next Follow-Up
Sally Jones	High conflict couples	12/1/2025	2	1	4/1/2026
Mike Everett	Teens, Families	11/2/2025	0	2	1/9/2026
Bernice Calls	LGBTQ, Religious Trauma	2/1/2024	0	4	1/3/2026

How to use this:
- Update after every professional interaction
- Review monthly to identify who needs follow-up
- Track both directions of referrals to see what's working
- Set reminders for quarterly check-ins with key contacts

EMAIL TEMPLATES FOR NETWORKING

Template 1: Initial Outreach

Subject: Would love to connect - [Your Specialty]

Hi [Name],

I came across your practice while researching [therapists/specialists] in the [location] area who work with [population]. Your work with [specific thing you noticed] really resonated with me.

I'm a [your credentials] specializing in [your niche]. I work privately with [your ideal clients] and am always looking to connect with other practitioners who serve similar populations.

Would you be open to a brief virtual coffee chat sometime in the next few weeks? I'd love to learn more about your practice and explore how we might support each other's clients.

Best, [Your Name] [Your Contact Info]

Template 2: Post-Coffee Chat Thank You

Subject: Thanks for connecting today

Hi [Name],

Thanks for taking the time to chat today. I really appreciated learning about your work with [specific detail they shared] and your approach to [something they mentioned].

I wanted to follow up with [resource/contact/information you offered].

I'm keeping you in mind for clients who might benefit from [their specialty], and I'm here as a resource anytime you have clients who might be a good fit for [your specialty].

Looking forward to staying connected.

[Your Name]

Template 3: Quarterly Check-In

Subject: Quick check-in from [Your Name]

Hi [Name],

Hope you've been well. I wanted to check in and let you know I'm currently accepting new clients for [your focus area/any new offerings].

If you come across anyone who might be a good fit, I'd be happy to talk with them. And as always, let me know if there's anything I can do to support your clients.

Hope to connect again soon.

[Your Name]

Template 4: Asking for Referrals (Without Feeling Gross)

Subject: Current availability for [Your Specialty]

Hi [Name],

I hope this finds you well. I wanted to reach out because I have a few openings in my practice right now for [specific type of client].

I know you work with [their population], and I'm wondering if you occasionally have clients who might benefit from [what you offer]. I'd love to be a resource if you come across anyone who seems like a good fit.

No pressure at all - just wanted to let you know I have capacity.
Thanks as always for being such a great colleague.

[Your Name]

Key principle: Frame it as "here's what I can offer" not "please send me clients because I'm desperate."

MONTHLY NETWORKING HABITS TRACKER

Build a sustainable networking practice - not a desperate sprint

This Month's Networking Goals:
- New connections to reach out to: _____
- Coffee chats to schedule: _____
- Networking events to attend: _____
- Follow-ups to send: _____

Weekly Networking Checklist:

Week 1:
- Reach out to 1-2 new potential connections
- Follow up with any recent coffee chats
- Share valuable content on professional platforms
- Update referral tracker

Week 2:
- Schedule 1 coffee chat
- Send quarterly check-in to 3-5 existing contacts
- Comment/engage on colleagues' posts
- Update referral tracker

Week 3:
- Attend 1 networking event (virtual or in-person)
- Follow up with people you met
- Send thank you notes
- Update referral tracker

Week 4:
- Review month's networking activities
- Assess what worked and what didn't
- Plan next month's networking focus
- Send any pending follow-ups

SCRIPTS FOR ASKING FOR REFERRALS

How to ask without feeling like you're begging

Script 1: At Networking Events
"I'm currently accepting new clients for [your specialty]. I work with [ideal client description]. f you come across anyone who might be a good fit, I'd love to connect with them."

Practice here:
_____
_____
_____
_____
_____

Script 2: In One-on-One Conversations
"I'd love to be a resource for your clients if you ever have someone who needs [your specialty]. What's the best way to make referrals to each other?"

Practice here:
_____
_____
_____
_____
_____

Script 3: When Someone Asks What You Do
"I'm a therapist specializing in [niche]. I work privately with [ideal clients] who are dealing with [specific issues]. I help them [outcome/transformation]."

Your version:
_____
_____
_____
_____
_____

Chapter 5 Action Items

Complete these within the next 7 days:
- Fill out the Coffee Chat Framework prep sheet for your next conversation
- Create or update your referral tracking system
- Send initial outreach emails to 3 potential networking contacts
- Schedule at least 1 coffee chat for this month
- Practice your networking introduction script out loud
- Set up a monthly reminder to review and update your referral tracker

REFLECTION QUESTIONS

Take 10 minutes to journal on these:

1. What feels uncomfortable about networking for you? Why?
   _____
   _____
   _____

2. Who are 5 people you'd genuinely enjoy connecting with professionally?
   _____
   _____
   _____

3. What value can you offer to your professional network (not just what you want to receive)?
   _____
   _____
   _____

4. What's one small networking action you can take THIS WEEK?
   _____
   _____
   _____

End of Chapter 5
Next: Chapter 6 - Innovative Service Delivery

Chapter 6

Innovative Service Delivery

You don't have to do 50-minute sessions forever.

Private pay gives you the freedom to design services that actually work for your clients AND your life.

Think about it: The 50-minute weekly session model was built for insurance billing, not for optimal outcomes. Some clients need more intensive work. Some need flexible scheduling. Some need something between "weekly therapy" and "see you when you're in crisis."

This chapter will help you:
- Explore service models beyond traditional weekly therapy
- Design packages and intensives that serve clients better
- Price and structure alternative offerings
- Decide what fits YOUR practice

You don't have to offer all of these. Pick what makes sense for your niche and your life.

Let's build services that actually help people transform.

SERVICE MENU BRAINSTORM

WHAT COULD YOU OFFER?
Traditional weekly therapy is ONE option. Here are others:

Intensive Sessions:
- 2-Hour Deep Dive Sessions
- Half-Day Intensives (3-4 Hours)
- Full-Day Intensives (6-8 Hours)
- Multi-Day Intensives (2-3 Days In A Row)

Packages:
- 6-Session Package Focused On Specific Outcome
- 12-Week Transformation Package
- Monthly Retainer For Ongoing Support
- Pre-Wedding Or Life Transition Package

Group Offerings:
- Therapy Groups (Ongoing Or Time-Limited)
- Psychoeducation Workshops
- Mastermind Or Support Groups
- Couples Or Family Intensives

Flexible Formats:
- Bi-Weekly Sessions With Longer Time (90 Min Every 2 Weeks)
- As-Needed Sessions (No Set Schedule)
- Combination Of Individual + Group
- Virtual + In-Person Hybrid

Specialized Services:
- Emdr Intensives
- Ketamine-Assisted Therapy Sessions
- Consultation For Professionals
- Clinical Supervision.

CHECK 3-5 OPTIONS THAT INTEREST YOU:
What excites you about these options?
_____
_____

What scares you about offering something different?
_____
_____
_____
_____
_____

CHOOSE YOUR SERVICE TO DEVELOP

YOU DON'T HAVE TO DO ALL OF THEM
Pick ONE service model to develop deeply right now.

WHICH ONE FITS YOUR PRACTICE BEST?

Consider:
- What your ideal clients actually need
- What you're trained/comfortable providing
- What fits your schedule and energy
- What you'd genuinely enjoy offering

THE SERVICE I'M GOING TO DEVELOP:
_____
_____
_____

WHY THIS ONE?
What problem does this solve for your clients?
_____
_____
_____
_____

Why is this a better fit than traditional weekly sessions?
_____
_____
_____
_____

What makes you qualified/excited to offer this?
_____
_____
_____
_____

For the rest of this chapter, we'll develop THIS service in detail.

You can always come back and develop others later.

DESIGNING YOUR SERVICE

LET'S BUILD THIS OUT

THE BASICS:
Service name: _____
Duration/format: _____

Example: "3-hour EMDR intensive" or "8-week anxiety breakthrough package"

WHO IS THIS FOR?
Ideal client for this specific service:
_____
_____
_____

What problem does this solve for them?
_____
_____
_____

What outcome will they get?
_____
_____
_____
_____

WHAT'S INCLUDED?
Be specific about what clients get:
- Number of sessions: _____
- Length of each session: _____
- Format (in-person, virtual, or both): _____
- Additional support between sessions? _____
- Worksheets/resources: _____
- Follow-up/check-ins: _____
- Other: _____

WHAT'S THE PROCESS?

How will sessions be structured?
Session 1:
_____
_____
_____
_____

Session 2-3 (or middle sessions):
_____
_____
_____
_____

Final session:
_____
_____
_____
_____

PRICING YOUR SERVICE

WHAT SHOULD YOU CHARGE?
Price based on what you need to sustain your practice, not what you think people will pay.

CALCULATE YOUR BASE PRICE:
Your hourly rate: $ _____
Total hours of direct client contact: _____
Base price (rate × hours): $ _____

ADD VALUE FOR:
- Preparation time: $ _____
- Materials/resources you'll create: $ _____
- Your specialized training: $ _____
- Follow-up support: $ _____
- Convenience/flexibility for client: $ _____

Total additional value: $ _____

YOUR PRICE:
Base price + additional value = $ _____
Does this feel aligned?
- Yes
- Too low
- Too high

If it feels off, what would feel right? $ _____

PAYMENT OPTIONS:
- Pay in full upfront
- Payment plan: _____ payments of $ _____ each
- Deposit required: $ _____ (then remaining $ _____ by _____)
- Other: _____

Remember: Packages and intensives are typically paid upfront or with a significant deposit. This protects your time.

LOGISTICS & BOUNDARIES

HOW WILL THIS ACTUALLY WORK?

SCHEDULING:
- How far in advance do clients need to book? _____
- How do they schedule? (link, email, phone) _____

Cancellation policy for this service:
_____
_____
_____
_____

If it's a package, what happens if they want to stop halfway through?
_____
_____
_____
_____

LOCATION/FORMAT:
Where will you provide this service?
- Your office
- Virtual only
- Hybrid (client chooses)
- Off-site location (retreat space, etc.)
- Other: _____

Do you need any special setup or equipment?
_____
_____
_____

BOUNDARIES:
Between-session contact for this service:
- None (sessions only)
- Email check-ins: _____
- Voxer/Marco Polo support: _____
- Emergency contact protocol: _____

Be clear about this upfront so clients know what to expect.

CONSENT & AGREEMENTS:

Do you need a separate agreement for this service?
- Yes
- No

What do clients need to know/agree to before starting?
_____
_____
_____
_____
_____

MARKETING YOUR NEW SERVICE

HOW WILL PEOPLE KNOW YOU OFFER THIS?

WEBSITE:
- Create a dedicated page for this service
- Add it to your services menu
- Update your homepage to mention it

What's the headline for this service on your website?
_____
_____
_____
_____

WHO WILL YOU TELL?
- Current clients (some may want to switch)
- Your email list
- Your referral network
- Social media followers
- Past clients who might benefit

Draft a simple announcement:

"I'm excited to offer [service name] for [ideal client]. This is perfect for [specific situation]. [Brief description of what it includes and the outcome they'll get]."

Your version:
_____
_____
_____
_____

REFERRAL LANGUAGE:
When networking, how will you describe this service?
_____
_____
_____
_____

TEST IT FIRST:
- Offer it to 1-3 clients at a beta price to refine the process
- Get feedback after each session
- Adjust as needed before full launch

Who are 2-3 people you could offer this to first?
1. _____
2. _____
3. _____

Chapter 6 Action Items

CHAPTER 6: WHAT YOU'VE CREATED
- Service menu brainstorm
- One service fully developed
- Pricing structure
- Logistics and boundaries
- Marketing plan

IMMEDIATE ACTION ITEMS:
- Create a dedicated page on your website for your new service offering
- Draft the service agreement or consent form
- Identify 2-3 beta clients to test this with
- Add this service to your consultation script (from Chapter 4)
- Update your professional intro to mention this offering when relevant
- Create a simple one-page PDF or Google Doc explaining the service that you can send to interested clients
- Tell your referral network about this new offering

REFLECTION:
What excites you most about offering this service?
_____
_____
_____

What's your biggest concern or hesitation?
_____
_____
_____

What needs to happen before you can launch this?
_____
_____
_____

When will you launch this service? _____

NEXT: Chapter 7 - CEO Mindset & Time Management
You've built the services. Now let's make sure you're running your practice like a business, not burning out.

Chapter 7

CEO Mindset & Time Management

You're not just a therapist anymore. You're a business owner.

That's a mindset shift most therapists never make. They stay stuck in "helper mode" - saying yes to everyone, undercharging, working evenings and weekends, and wondering why they're burned out.

Private pay requires you to think like a CEO:
- Your time has value
- Not every client is the right client
- Systems matter more than hustle
- Boundaries protect your business
- Profit isn't a dirty word

This chapter will help you:
- Shift from employee mindset to CEO mindset
- Manage your time like the valuable resource it is
- Build systems that keep you from burning out
- Track the numbers that actually matter

You can't help anyone if you're exhausted and resentful.
Let's build a practice that sustains you.

MINDSET SHIFT INVENTORY

FROM EMPLOYEE TO CEO
Check which mindset you're currently operating from:

EMPLOYEE MINDSET:
- I should be available whenever clients need me
- I feel guilty about my rates
- I say yes to clients even when they're not the right fit
- I work evenings and weekends because that's when people need therapy
- I don't track my finances closely
- I feel bad about making a profit
- I'm afraid to raise my rates
- I do everything myself because it's easier than delegating

CEO MINDSET:
- I have clear boundaries around my availability
- I charge what I need to sustain my practice and my life
- I refer out clients who aren't the right fit
- I design my schedule around my life, not the other way around
- I know my numbers and make decisions based on data
- Profit means sustainability and allows me to serve clients better
- I raise rates regularly to keep pace with expenses and growth
- I invest in systems and support that free up my time

WHICH SHIFT DO YOU MOST NEED TO MAKE?

What's one belief you need to let go of?
_____
_____
_____
_____

What's one new belief you're choosing to adopt?
_____
_____
_____
_____

TIME AUDIT

WHERE DOES YOUR TIME ACTUALLY GO?
You can't manage what you don't measure.

Track your time for ONE WEEK. Be honest.

DIRECT CLIENT WORK:
Sessions: _____ hours
Consultation calls: _____ hours
Notes/documentation: _____ hours
Total: _____ hours

ADMIN/OPERATIONS:
Email: _____ hours
Scheduling: _____ hours
Billing/insurance: _____ hours
Phone calls: _____ hours
Total: _____ hours

BUSINESS DEVELOPMENT:
Marketing: _____ hours
Networking: _____ hours
Website/social media: _____ hours
Learning/training: _____ hours
Total: _____ hours

OTHER:
Meetings: _____ hours
Miscellaneous: _____ hours
Total: _____ hours

TOTAL HOURS WORKED THIS WEEK: _____

WHAT DO YOU NOTICE?
What's taking more time than it should?
_____
_____
_____
_____

What could be automated, delegated, or eliminated?
_____
_____
_____
_____

What are you avoiding that you should be doing more of?
_____
_____
_____
_____
_____

YOUR IDEAL WEEK

DESIGN YOUR WEEK INTENTIONALLY
Stop letting your schedule happen TO you.

IDEAL CLIENT-FACING HOURS:
How many client sessions per week do you WANT to do? _____

What days do you want to see clients?
- Monday
- Tuesday
- Wednesday
- Thursday
- Friday

What times work best for you?
- Morning (before 12pm)
- Afternoon (12-5pm)
- Evening (after 5pm)

YOUR IDEAL WEEKLY SCHEDULE:

	MONDAY	TUESDAY	WEDNESDAY	THURSDAY	FRIDAY
9-12am					
12-3pm					
3-6pm					
6-9pm					

Fill in: C = Clients, A = Admin, M = Marketing, O = Off

NON-NEGOTIABLE TIME BLOCKS:
- Admin day/half-day: _____
- Marketing time: _____
- No-meeting time: _____
- Business development: _____
- Personal time (lunch, workout, etc.): _____

BOUNDARIES:
Latest session you'll schedule: _____
Days you don't work: _____
Maximum clients per day: _____
Buffer time between sessions: _____

YOUR FINANCIAL DASHBOARD

THE NUMBERS YOU NEED TO KNOW
You don't need complicated accounting. You need these basics.

MONTHLY REVENUE:
Gross revenue (total income): $ _____
Number of sessions: _____
Average session rate: $ _____

MONTHLY EXPENSES:
Rent/office: $ _____
EHR/software: $ _____
Insurance (malpractice, etc.): $ _____
Marketing: $ _____
Continuing education: $ _____
Professional memberships: $ _____
Phone/internet: $ _____
Other: $ _____
Total monthly expenses: $ _____

NET INCOME:
Gross revenue - expenses = $ _____

KEY METRICS TO TRACK:
How many sessions do you need per month to break even? _____
How many to hit your income goal? _____
Current utilization rate (sessions filled vs. available): _____%

QUARTERLY CHECK-IN:
- Q1 revenue: $ _____ Sessions: _____
- Q2 revenue: $ _____ Sessions: _____
- Q3 revenue: $ _____ Sessions: _____
- Q4 revenue: $ _____ Sessions: _____

Are you on track?
- Yes
- No
- Need to adjust

What needs to change?
_____
_____
_____
_____
_____

SYSTEMS THAT SAVE YOU TIME

AUTOMATE WHAT YOU CAN
Stop doing manually what technology can handle.

SCHEDULING:
- Use online scheduling (Calendly, Practice Better, SimplePractice, etc.)
- Automated appointment reminders
- Automated waitlist management
- Self-scheduling for established clients

BILLING/PAYMENTS:
- Auto-charge credit cards on file
- Automated invoices
- Automated superbill generation
- Payment plans set up in advance

MARKETING:
- Email welcome sequence
- Scheduled social media posts
- Automated consultation booking
- FAQ page to answer common questions

ADMIN:
- Note templates in your EHR
- Canned email responses for common questions
- Digital intake forms
- Automated file organization

WHAT DO YOU NEED TO SET UP OR IMPROVE?
Top 3 systems to implement this quarter:
1. _____
2. _____
3. _____

WHAT COULD YOU OUTSOURCE?
- Bookkeeping
- Website maintenance
- Social media management
- Virtual assistant for scheduling/admin
- Billing/superbill creation

What's worth paying someone else to do?
_____
_____
_____
_____
_____

AVOIDING BURNOUT

YOU CAN'T POUR FROM AN EMPTY CUP
Private pay gives you freedom. Use it.

WARNING SIGNS YOU'RE HEADING FOR BURNOUT:
- Dreading sessions with clients
- Working through lunch or staying late regularly
- Checking email on weekends/evenings
- Feeling resentful about your schedule
- Constantly tired or getting sick
- Canceling personal plans for work
- Not taking time off
- Difficulty disconnecting from work

How many did you check? _____

If it's more than 2-3, something needs to change NOW.

YOUR SUSTAINABILITY PLAN:

Non-negotiable self-care practices:

Time off you're committing to:
- One day off per week (minimum)
- One full weekend per month
- ____ weeks of vacation per year

Maximum caseload: _____ clients
Maximum sessions per day: _____
Maximum days per week seeing clients: _____

WHAT DRAINS YOU?
Clients/situations that drain your energy:

How will you handle these going forward?
- Refer out
- Raise rates for difficult clients

- Limit number of these cases
- Add buffer time after draining sessions
- Other: _____

WHAT ENERGIZES YOU?
The work that lights you up:

How can you do MORE of this?
_____
_____
_____
_____
_____

Chapter 7 Action Items

CHAPTER 7: WHAT YOU'VE CREATED
- Mindset shift inventory
- Time audit
- Ideal week design
- Financial dashboard
- Systems assessment
- Burnout prevention plan

IMMEDIATE ACTION ITEMS:
- Track your time for one full week (use your phone timer or a simple spreadsheet)
- Calculate your current monthly revenue and expenses
- Identify ONE system you can automate this month
- Block out your ideal schedule in your calendar for next month
- Set up one non-negotiable boundary you've been avoiding
- Schedule your time off for the next 6 months
- Review your current caseload and identify any clients who aren't the right fit

REFLECTION:
What's the biggest shift you need to make to think like a CEO?
_____
_____
_____
_____

What's one boundary you're committing to starting NOW?
_____
_____
_____
_____

What would your practice look like if you weren't burned out?
_____
_____
_____
_____

NEXT: Chapter 8 - Client Retention & Ethical Offboarding

You know how to run your business sustainably. Now let's talk about keeping the right clients and gracefully ending with the wrong ones.

Chapter 8

Client Retention & Ethical Offboarding

Not every client is meant to stay forever.

Some clients graduate. Some clients plateau. Some clients aren't the right fit and never were.

Knowing when to keep working and when to end is a skill most therapists struggle with.

We hold on too long because we don't want to "abandon" them. Or we end too abruptly because we're burned out and don't know how to have the conversation.

This chapter will help you:
- Recognize when it's time to end therapy
- Have the offboarding conversation without guilt
- Create ethical closure for clients
- Build a referral network for transitions
- Retain the right clients longer

Good endings create good referrals. Let's make sure you know how to do both.

THE RETENTION DECISION FRAMEWORK
How do you know when it's time to end therapy with a client?

CHECK ALL THAT APPLY:
- Client has met their treatment goals
- Client has plateaued and isn't making progress
- Client keeps canceling or no-showing
- Client isn't engaging in the work
- Client needs a higher level of care than you can provide
- Client needs a different specialty than you offer
- Client is beyond your scope of practice
- The therapeutic relationship isn't working
- You dread sessions with this client
- Client can't afford your rate and it's causing strain
- Client is consistently disrespectful or violates boundaries
- You're not the right fit for what they need

IF YOU CHECKED 1-2: Have a conversation about progress and goals
IF YOU CHECKED 3-4: It's probably time to transition or refer out
IF YOU CHECKED 5+: It's definitely time to end

REFLECTION:
Is there a client you're currently working with who fits this list?
_____
_____
_____
_____

What's kept you from having the conversation?
_____
_____
_____
_____

What do they actually need that you're not providing?
_____
_____
_____

THE OFFBOARDING CONVERSATION

HOW TO END THERAPY GRACEFULLY
This doesn't have to be dramatic or guilt-inducing.

THE BASIC SCRIPT:
"I've been thinking about our work together, and I want to check in with you about where we are. [Acknowledge progress they've made]. I'm wondering if it might be time to [graduate/transition/take a break]. What are your thoughts?"

WHEN THEY'VE MET THEIR GOALS:
"You've made incredible progress since we started. You came in struggling with [original presenting problem], and now you're [current state]. I'm wondering if you feel ready to wrap up our work together, or if there's something else you want to focus on?"

WHEN THEY'VE PLATEAUED:
"I've noticed we've been covering similar ground for the past few weeks/months. I want to make sure therapy is still serving you. Sometimes a break or a different approach can be helpful. What do you think?"

WHEN THEY NEED SOMETHING DIFFERENT:
"Based on what you've shared, I think you might benefit from [specific type of therapy/specialist/level of care]. I want to make sure you're getting the best support possible, and I think [referral] might be a better fit for what you need right now."

WHEN IT'S NOT WORKING:
"I want to be honest with you. I don't think I'm the right therapist for what you need. That doesn't mean therapy won't help - it just means you might benefit from working with someone who [specializes in X/uses a different approach/etc.]. I want to help you find someone who's a better fit."

YOUR VERSION:
Write the script for a client you need to transition:

_____
_____
_____
_____
_____
_____
_____
_____

HANDLING DIFFICULT ENDINGS

WHAT IF THEY DON'T WANT TO END?
Sometimes clients resist ending even when it's clearly time.

IF THEY PUSH BACK:
"I hear that this feels scary. Ending therapy can bring up a lot of feelings. Let's talk about what's coming up for you."

Then explore:
- What are they afraid will happen if they stop?
- What skills have they built that they can use on their own?
- What support do they have outside of therapy?

OFFER A TRANSITION PLAN:
- Spacing out sessions (biweekly, then monthly, then as-needed)
- Set a specific number of remaining sessions
- Schedule a check-in in 3-6 months
- Keep the door open for future sessions if needed

Your transition plan:
_____
_____
_____
_____

IF THEY'RE ANGRY:
Stay calm and professional. Don't defend yourself or over-explain.

"I understand you're upset. This is my professional recommendation based on what I think will serve you best. If you'd like to continue therapy, I'm happy to help you find someone else."

IF THEY GHOST:
Send one final email:

"Hi [Name], I haven't heard from you in [timeframe]. I'm assuming you've decided to discontinue therapy, which is completely fine. If you'd like to schedule a final session for closure, let me know. Otherwise, I'll go ahead and close your file. Wishing you all the best."
Don't chase them. Close the file and move on.

BUILDING YOUR REFERRAL NETWORK

WHO DO YOU REFER TO?
You can't be everything to everyone. Build a solid referral list.

THERAPISTS FOR DIFFERENT SPECIALTIES:
Trauma (if not your specialty): _____
Eating disorders: _____
Substance use: _____
Couples therapy: _____
Child/adolescent: _____
EMDR: _____
DBT: _____
Other: _____

LOWER-COST OPTIONS:
Sliding scale therapists: _____
Community mental health: _____
Training clinics: _____
Online therapy platforms: _____

HIGHER LEVEL OF CARE:
IOP programs: _____
Residential treatment: _____
Psychiatric hospitals: _____
Crisis services: _____

OTHER RESOURCES:
Support groups: _____
Coaches (if therapy isn't the right fit): _____
Psychiatrists for medication: _____

KEEP THIS LIST UPDATED:
- Review quarterly
- Add new contacts as you meet them
- Remove providers who are no longer practicing
- Ask for feedback from clients you've referred

When was the last time you updated your referral list? _____

RETAINING THE RIGHT CLIENTS

HOW TO KEEP GOOD CLIENTS ENGAGED
Retention isn't about keeping everyone forever. It's about keeping the RIGHT clients for the RIGHT length of time.

CHECK-IN QUESTIONS TO ASK REGULARLY:
- "How is therapy feeling for you right now?"
- "Are we working on what matters most to you?"
- "What's been most helpful? What hasn't been helpful?"
- "Is there anything we should be doing differently?"

Ask these every 3-4 months, or when you notice engagement dropping.

SIGNS A CLIENT IS LOSING ENGAGEMENT:
- More last-minute cancellations
- Less talkative in sessions
- Vague responses to questions
- Not doing any between-session work
- Sessions feel flat or repetitive

If you notice these signs, address it directly:
"I've noticed [specific behavior]. I'm wondering what's going on for you. Are we still working on the right things? Is therapy still helpful?"

HOW TO KEEP SESSIONS FRESH:
- Revisit goals regularly and update them
- Try new approaches or interventions
- Assign between-session experiments
- Bring in new resources (books, podcasts, worksheets)
- Ask what THEY think would be helpful

Don't just keep doing the same thing because it's comfortable.

WHEN TO SUGGEST A BREAK:
Sometimes clients need to take a break and come back later. That's okay.

"It seems like you've made a lot of progress and might benefit from some time to practice what you've learned on your own. What if we took a break for [timeframe] and then checked in? You can always reach out sooner if you need to."

This gives them permission to leave AND come back without guilt.

Private Pay Practitioners Workbook

CLOSURE & FINAL SESSIONS

HOW TO DO A GOOD FINAL SESSION
Don't just end therapy without acknowledging the work you've done together.

STRUCTURE FOR A FINAL SESSION:

1. **REFLECT ON PROGRESS**
   "When we started, you were [original presenting problem]. Now you're [current state]. What stands out to you about the progress you've made?"

   Let them reflect first, then add your observations.

2. **REVIEW SKILLS & STRATEGIES**
   "What are the tools or strategies you've learned that have been most helpful?"

   Remind them of what they can use going forward.

3. **ANTICIPATE FUTURE CHALLENGES**
   "What situations might be tough for you in the future? How will you handle them?"

   Help them think ahead so they feel prepared.

4. **NORMALIZE RETURNS**
   "It's completely normal to come back to therapy in the future if you need to You're not starting over - you're building on what you've already done."

5. **EXPRESS APPRECIATION**
   "It's been a privilege to work with you. I'm grateful you trusted me with your story."

   Keep it genuine and brief.

YOUR FINAL SESSION OUTLINE:
What will you say/do in a final session?

_____
_____
_____
_____
_____
_____
_____
_____

Chapter 8 Action Items

CHAPTER 8: WHAT YOU'VE CREATED
- Retention decision framework
- Offboarding conversation scripts
- Difficult endings protocol
- Referral network list
- Client engagement strategies
- Final session structure

IMMEDIATE ACTION ITEMS:
- Update your referral list with current contact information
- Identify 1-2 clients who might be ready to end or transition
- Practice your offboarding script out loud
- Schedule check-ins with current clients to assess engagement
- Create a simple termination letter template for your files
- Add "final session" to your calendar when a client decides to end
- Follow up with any clients who ghosted (send closure email)

REFLECTION:
Who is one client you need to have an offboarding conversation with?
_____
_____
_____
_____

What's been stopping you?
_____
_____
_____
_____

What's one thing you'll do differently in your next ending?
_____
_____
_____

NEXT: Chapter 9 - Scaling Your Impact
You know how to bring clients in and end well. Now let's talk about growing your practice and your income without burning out.

Chapter 9

Scaling Your Impact

You've built your practice. Now what?

Scaling doesn't mean seeing more clients. It means making more impact (and more income) without trading more hours.

You can't scale a practice by just adding more sessions. There are only so many hours in a week, and you'll burn out fast if that's your only strategy.

This chapter will help you:
- Think beyond one-on-one sessions
- Build multiple revenue streams
- Create systems that allow you to grow sustainably
- Plan for the next phase of your practice

Scaling is about leverage - doing more with the infrastructure you've already built.

Let's design a practice that grows without consuming your life.

REVENUE STREAM IDEAS

BEYOND ONE-ON-ONE SESSIONS
How else can you generate income from your expertise?

DIRECT CLIENT SERVICES:
- Group therapy
- Workshops or intensives
- Online courses
- Membership community
- Coaching programs
- Consultation packages

PRODUCTS:
- Workbooks or journals
- Templates or worksheets
- Recorded trainings
- Digital downloads
- Books or ebooks

PROFESSIONAL SERVICES:
- Clinical supervision
- Consultation for other therapists
- Speaking engagements
- Training programs
- Continuing education courses

PASSIVE INCOME:
- Affiliate partnerships (therapy tools, books, etc.)
- Online courses (pre-recorded)
- Membership site
- Licensed content

WHICH 2-3 INTEREST YOU MOST?

1. Why:
   _____
   _____
   _____
   _____

Private Pay Practitioners Workbook

2. Why:
_____
_____
_____
_____

3. Why:
_____
_____
_____
_____
_____

WHAT WOULD IT TAKE TO LAUNCH ONE OF THESE?

Pick ONE to develop:
Revenue stream: _____

What you need to create:
_____
_____
_____
_____

Timeline to launch: _____
Projected income (realistic): _____

_____

SEASONAL STRATEGY

PLAN FOR THE RHYTHM OF THE YEAR
Private pay practices have natural ebbs and flows. Plan for them.

BUSY SEASONS (when to take on more clients):
- January (New Year momentum)
- September (back-to-school energy)
- After major holidays when people realize they need support

Your busiest months: _____

SLOW SEASONS (when to focus on other things):
- Summer (vacations, schedules disrupted)
- Late November/December (holidays)
- Spring break periods

Your slowest months: _____

QUARTERLY PLANNING:

Q1 (January-March):
Focus:
_____
_____
_____
_____

Revenue goal: _____

Key projects:
_____
_____
_____
_____

Q2 (April-June):
Focus:
_____
_____
_____

Revenue goal: _____
Key projects:
_____
_____
_____
_____

Q3 (July-September):
Focus:
_____
_____

Revenue goal: _____
Key projects:
_____
_____
_____
_____

Q4 (October-December):
Focus:
_____
_____
_____
_____

Revenue goal: _____
Key projects:
_____
_____
_____
_____

BUILDING A TEAM

YOU DON'T HAVE TO DO THIS ALONE
At some point, you might want help. Here's what that could look like.

ROLES YOU MIGHT HIRE FOR:
- Virtual assistant (scheduling, admin, email management)
- Bookkeeper (finances, taxes, invoicing)
- Marketing support (social media, website, content)
- Billing specialist (insurance, superbills)
- Associate therapist (if you want to grow beyond yourself)
- Receptionist/intake coordinator
- IT support (tech issues, EMR setup)

WHAT DO YOU NEED HELP WITH MOST?
Top 3 tasks you'd love to outsource:
1. _____
2. _____
3. _____

WHEN WILL YOU HIRE?
- When I'm consistently booked and turning away clients
- When I'm spending more than 10 hours/week on admin
- When I want to add a new revenue stream but don't have time
- When I'm burned out and need support
- Other: _____

What's your revenue threshold for hiring? $ _____

BUDGET FOR HELP:
How much could you invest per month in support? $ _____

What would that buy you?
_____
_____

Is the ROI worth it?
- Yes
- Not yet
- Need to think about it

DECIDING TO GROW (OR NOT)

SCALING ISN'T FOR EVERYONE
Some therapists want a solo practice. That's completely valid.

SOLO PRACTICE:
- You see 15-25 clients per week
- You handle everything yourself (or outsource admin only)
- Income is capped by your available hours
- Full control over your schedule and clients
- Simplicity and autonomy

GROUP PRACTICE:
- You hire other therapists
- You become more business owner, less clinician
- Income potential increases (leverage)
- More complexity and management
- Team to support and collaborate with

WHICH FEELS RIGHT FOR YOU?

Solo practice forever
Solo for now, maybe grow later
Want to build a group practice
Not sure yet

IF YOU WANT TO STAY SOLO:
How will you maximize income without adding more sessions?
_____
_____
_____
_____

What will you offer beyond traditional therapy?
_____
_____
_____
_____

IF YOU WANT TO GROW A GROUP PRACTICE:
What's your timeline? _____
How many therapists do you want? _____

What type of therapists will you hire?
_____
_____
_____
_____

What's your vision for this practice?
_____
_____
_____
_____

YOUR LEGACY PRACTICE

WHAT DO YOU WANT THIS TO BECOME?
Think 3-5 years out. What does your practice look like?

YOUR PRACTICE IN 3-5 YEARS:
Number of clients you're seeing per week: _____

Types of services you offer:
_____
_____
_____
_____

Revenue streams:
_____
_____
_____
_____

Team members (if any):
_____
_____
_____
_____

YOUR LIFE IN 3-5 YEARS:
How many hours per week are you working? _____

What does your schedule look like?
_____
_____
_____
_____

What are you doing outside of work?
_____
_____
_____
_____

What has changed from where you are now?
_____
_____
_____
_____
_____
_____
_____

YOUR IMPACT:
Who are you helping?
_____
_____
_____
_____

What problem are you solving?
_____
_____
_____
_____

What are you known for?
_____
_____
_____
_____
_____

WHAT COULD GO WRONG?

PLAN FOR OBSTACLES
Every business faces challenges. Here's how to prepare.

POTENTIAL OBSTACLES:
- Slow months with low revenue
- Unexpected expenses
- Burnout or health issues

- Market saturation in your area
- Changes in insurance/regulations
- Technology failures
- Bad reviews or reputation issues
- Competition from online therapy platforms
- Personal life changes (moving, family, etc.)

YOUR BACKUP PLANS:
Financial buffer: How many months of expenses do you have saved? _____
If revenue drops 50% for 3 months, what would you do?
_____
_____
_____
_____

If you couldn't see clients for 6 weeks, how would you manage?
_____
_____
_____
_____

BUSINESS INSURANCE:
- Malpractice insurance (obviously)
- Business owner's policy
- Disability insurance
- Liability insurance for your space
- Cyber liability insurance

Do you have adequate coverage?
- Yes
- Need to review
- Need to get

RISK MANAGEMENT:
What's your biggest business risk right now?
_____
_____
_____

How will you mitigate it?
_____
_____
_____
_____

Chapter 9 Action Items

CHAPTER 9: WHAT YOU'VE CREATED
- 90-day action plan
- Revenue stream ideas
- Seasonal strategy
- Team/hiring plan
- Growth decision
- Legacy practice vision
- Risk management plan

IMMEDIATE ACTION ITEMS:
- Put your 90-day priorities in your calendar with specific deadlines
- Set up your 30/60/90 day review dates
- Research ONE new revenue stream you want to test
- Map out your quarterly focuses for the year
- Calculate your financial buffer and set a savings goal
- Decide if you're staying solo or planning to grow
- Share your 90-day plan with your accountability partner

REFLECTION:
What excites you most about the next phase of your practice?

_____
_____
_____
_____
_____
_____
_____
_____
_____

What scares you?

_____
_____
_____
_____
_____
_____
_____
_____
_____

What's the ONE thing you're committing to doing in the next 30 days?
___
___
___
___
___
___
___

NEXT: Conclusion - Your Next 30 Days (p. 103)
You've done the work. Now it's time to actually implement.

CONCLUSION

Your 90-Day Action Plan

YOU'VE DONE THE WORK.

NOW DO THE WORK.

You've filled out this entire workbook. That's more than most people do.

But let's be honest: Nothing changes if you don't actually implement what you've created here.

This isn't a workbook you finish and put on a shelf. This is your operating manual for building a private pay practice that actually works.

The next 90 days are critical.

Most people get excited, make plans, and then... nothing. Life happens. Clients need you. Admin piles up. And suddenly it's three months later and nothing has changed.

Don't be like most people.

This conclusion will help you:
- Identify your immediate next steps
- Build momentum in the first 90 days
- Set up accountability that actually works
- Celebrate progress along the way

Private pay isn't a dream. It's a decision followed by consistent action.

Let's make sure you actually do this.

YOUR 90-DAY ACTION PLAN

WHAT ARE YOU ACTUALLY GOING TO DO?
You've been through this entire workbook. Now it's time to commit to action.

Pick your TOP 3 PRIORITIES for the next 90 days.

PRIORITY #1:

What:
_____
_____
_____
_____

Why this matters:
_____
_____
_____
_____

Action steps:
Week 1-2:
_____
_____
_____
_____

Week 3-4:
_____
_____
_____
_____

Week 5-6:
_____
_____
_____
_____

Week 7-8:
_____
_____
_____
_____

Week 9-10:
_____
_____
_____
_____

Week 11-12:
_____
_____
_____
_____

Success metric:
_____
_____

PRIORITY #2:
What:
_____
_____
_____
_____

Why this matters:
_____
_____
_____
_____

Action steps:
Week 1-2:
_____
_____
_____
_____

Week 3-4:
_____
_____
_____
_____

Week 5-6:
_____
_____
_____
_____

Week 7-8:
_____
_____
_____
_____

Week 9-10:
_____
_____
_____
_____

Week 11-12:
_____
_____
_____
_____

Success metric:
_____
_____
_____
_____

PRIORITY #3:

What:
___
___
___

Why this matters:
___
___
___
___

Action steps:

Week 1-2:
___
___
___

Week 3-4:
___
___
___

Week 5-6:
___
___
___

Week 7-8:
___
___
___

Week 9-10:
___

Week 11-12:

Success metric:

WHAT WILL YOU STOP DOING?
To make room for your priorities, you need to let go of things that aren't serving you.

THINGS TO ELIMINATE:

THINGS TO DELEGATE OR OUTSOURCE:

THINGS TO PUT ON HOLD FOR NOW:

ACCOUNTABILITY:
Who will hold you accountable?

How often will you check in?
_____
_____

How will you track progress?
_____
_____
_____

OBSTACLES YOU'LL FACE:
What will try to derail you in the next 90 days?
_____
_____
_____
_____
_____
_____

How will you handle these obstacles?
_____
_____
_____
_____
_____
_____

REVIEW DATES:
30-day check-in: _____
60-day check-in: _____
90-day review: _____
_____

FINAL WORDS

YOU'VE GOT THIS.

You made it through this entire workbook. That's not nothing.

Most therapists never do the work to build a private pay practice. They think about it. They dream about it. They complain about insurance.

But they don't actually do anything.

You're different. You've invested time, energy, and thought into this.

Now it's time to implement.

HERE'S THE TRUTH:

Your first consultation won't be perfect.

Your website won't be perfect.

Your rates won't feel comfortable right away.

Your networking will feel awkward.

You'll doubt yourself.

Do it anyway.

PRIVATE PAY ISN'T A DREAM. IT'S A DECISION.

You've made the decision. Now take action.

Imperfect action beats perfect planning every single time.

Start with ONE thing from this workbook. Just one.

Then do the next thing. And the next.

That's how practices are built.

You don't need more information. You need implementation.

This workbook is your roadmap. Now go.

You've got this.

DJ

APPENDIX

Quick Reference & Resources

APPENDIX INTRO

QUICK REFERENCE & RESOURCES

This section includes:
- Essential implementation timeline
- Troubleshooting guide
- Resource links
- Notes pages for your practice planning

ESSENTIAL IMPLEMENTATION TIMELINE

YOUR FIRST 90 DAYS IN PRIVATE PAY

Use this as a guide, not a rigid rule.

DAYS 1-7: FOUNDATION
- Complete your ideal client avatar
- Write your Why statement
- Update website with new messaging
- Set your rates
- Create consultation booking system

DAYS 8-14: VISIBILITY
- Update all online listings (Psychology Today, Google, etc.)
- Post on social media (use your 30-day plan)
- Reach out to 5 people in your network
- Schedule 2 coffee chats

DAYS 15-21: SYSTEMS
- Set up automated scheduling
- Create intake forms
- Build consultation script
- Organize referral list
- Set up payment processing

DAYS 22-30: MOMENTUM
- Have first consultations
- Start first private pay clients
- Follow up with networking contacts
- Track your numbers
- Adjust what's not working

DAYS 31-60: CONSISTENCY
- Continue marketing weekly
- Network monthly
- Refine consultation script based on feedback
- Add one new service offering
- Build financial buffer

DAYS 61-90: OPTIMIZATION
- Review what's working
- Raise rates if needed
- Delegate or automate one task
- Plan next quarter
- Celebrate wins

WHERE ARE YOU IN THIS TIMELINE?
Current day: _____
What's your next milestone? _____
What needs to happen this week? _____

TROUBLESHOOTING GUIDE

COMMON PROBLEMS & SOLUTIONS

PROBLEM: No one is booking consultations
POSSIBLE CAUSES:
- Website doesn't clearly explain what you do
- Consultation link is hard to find
- You're not actively marketing
- Your niche is too broad
- People don't know you exist

SOLUTIONS:
→ Review Chapter 3 (messaging)
→ Make booking link prominent on every page
→ Post consistently for 30 days
→ Narrow your niche
→ Tell your network you're taking clients

PROBLEM: Consultations aren't converting to clients
POSSIBLE CAUSES:
- Not pre-qualifying before booking
- Script feels salesy or awkward
- Not addressing their specific problem
- Pricing not discussed clearly
- Not asking for the commitment

SOLUTIONS:
→ Add pre-qualifying questions to booking form
→ Practice script until it feels natural (Chapter 4)
→ Focus on their outcome, not your credentials
→ State your rate confidently
→ End with: "Would you like to get started?"

PROBLEM: Clients keep canceling or no-showing
POSSIBLE CAUSES:
- No cancellation policy
- Not charging for late cancellations
- Wrong clients in your practice
- No automated reminders

SOLUTIONS:
→ Create and enforce cancellation policy
→ Charge for late cancels/no-shows
→ Pre-qualify better (Chapter 4)
→ Set up automated 24-hour reminders

PROBLEM: Fully booked but still struggling financially
POSSIBLE CAUSES:
- Rates too low
- Too many sliding scale clients
- High expenses
- Not tracking numbers

SOLUTIONS:
→ Raise rates immediately
→ Limit sliding scale spots
→ Review expenses (Chapter 7)
→ Use financial dashboard weekly

PROBLEM: Burned out and resentful
POSSIBLE CAUSES:
- No boundaries
- Wrong clients
- Working too many hours
- No time off
- Doing everything yourself

SOLUTIONS:
→ Review Chapter 7 (boundaries)
→ Refer out misfit clients (Chapter 8)
→ Reduce session availability
→ Schedule time off NOW
→ Delegate admin tasks

RESOURCES

TOOLS & RESOURCES FOR PRIVATE PAY PRACTICE

PRACTICE MANAGEMENT / EMR:
- SimplePractice
- TherapyNotes
- Practice Better
- Jane App
- My Clients Plus

SCHEDULING:
- Calendly
- Acuity Scheduling
- Google Calendar (free)

PAYMENT PROCESSING:
- Stripe
- Square
- Ivy Pay
- PayPal

WEBSITE BUILDERS:
- Brighter Vision (therapy-specific)
- Squarespace
- WordPress
- Wix

MARKETING:
- Psychology Today directory

- Google Business Profile (free)
- Therapy Tribe
- GoodTherapy
- Mental Health Match
- Therapy for Black Girls
- Therapy Den
- Inclusive Therapy
- Zencare
- National Queer & Trans Therapists of Color Network
- Local SEO services

BOOKKEEPING:
- QuickBooks
- Wave (free)
- FreshBooks
- Hire a bookkeeper (worth it)

LEARNING & COMMUNITY:
- Private Pay Practitioners Patreon (patreon.com/privatepay)
- Black Private Pay Practitioners on Facebook
- Private Practice Skills podcast
- The Abundance Practice podcast
- Practice of Therapy podcast

BUSINESS LEGAL:
- LegalZoom (LLC formation)
- Rocket Lawyer
- Local business attorney
- CPA for tax planning

RECOMMENDED READING:

"The Private Pay Practitioners Playbook" by DJ Burr, LMHC, LPC

"Profit First" by Mike Michalowicz

"Profit First for Therapists" by Julie Herres

"The E-Myth Revisited" by Michael Gerber

"Building Your Ideal Private Practice" by Lynn Grodzki

"The Money Mindset Fix" by Brad Klontz

DISCLAIMER:

These are resources I've found helpful or that other practitioners recommend. I don't receive compensation for these recommendations (unless otherwise noted). Do your own research before investing.

NOTES: WEBSITE & MESSAGING

WEBSITE & MESSAGING NOTES
Use this space for brainstorming, drafts, and ideas.

NOTES: CONSULTATION & CLIENT JOURNEY

CONSULTATION & CLIENT JOURNEY NOTES
Use this space for brainstorming, drafts, and ideas.

NOTES: NETWORKING & REFERRALS

NETWORKING & REFERRALS NOTES
Use this space for tracking contacts, conversation notes, and follow-ups.

NOTES: PRACTICE PLANNING

PRACTICE PLANNING NOTES
Use this space for goals, ideas, and future planning.

THIS IS YOUR PRACTICE.

You get to design it however you want.

Use this workbook.

Come back to it.

Revise your answers as you grow.

This isn't a one-time exercise.

It's a living document for your business.

Keep building.

You've got this. I know you know it, too.

Thank you for being here.

With admiration,

DJ Burr

www.ingramcontent.com/pod-product-compliance
Lightning Source LLC
Chambersburg PA
CBHW080518030426
42337CB00023B/4563